melt & mold
soap
crafting

melt & mold
soap
crafting

C. Kaila Westerman

STOREY BOOKS

North Adams

Massachusetts

The mission of Storey Communications is to serve our customers by publishing practical information that encourages personal independence in harmony with the environment.

Edited by Deborah Balmuth and Robin Catalano
Cover design by Meredith Maker
Cover and interior photographs by Giles Prett
Additional photos by © Jeff Burke and Lorraine Triolo for Artville;
© Joe Atlas for Artville; © Eyewire Images; © PhotoDisc, Inc.
Art direction, text design and production by Mark Tomasi
Project photo styling by Robin Brickman
Additional photo styling by Mark Tomasi
Indexed by Nan Badgett/Word•a•bil•i•ty

The information in this book is true and complete to the best of our knowledge. All recommendations are made without guarantee on the part of the author or Storey Books. The author and publisher disclaim any liability in connection with the use of this information. For additional information, please contact Storey Books, 210 MASS MoCA Way, North Adams, MA 01247.

Storey books are available for special premium and promotional uses and for customized editions. For further information, please call Storey's Custom Publishing Department at (800) 793-9396.

Printed in the United States by Banta Book Group, Menasha, WI
10 9 8 7 6 5 4 3

Library of Congress Cataloging-in-Publication Data

Westerman, C. Kaila (Carolyn Kaila), 1959–
     Melt & mold soap crafting / C. Kaila Westerman.
         p.   cm.
     Includes index
     ISBN 1-58017-293-8 (pbk. : alk. paper)
     1. Soap. I. Title: Melt and mold soap crafting. II. Title.
TP991 .W48 2000
668'.12—dc21
                                                                     00-039494
                                                                     CIP

contents

Dedication

Thank you to Phyllis and Richard Westerman for instilling in me a love of hard work and a spirit of self-confidence, independence, peace, and self-worth. You have been great parents from the first.

Acknowledgments

Many thanks to my loving and supportive family and soap-crafting friends: my husband, Trung Bui, and business associates Lora Juge, Susan Slovensky, Janie and Dennis Gray, Gail Matsuura, Tom and Glinda Bauer, Senna Antrium, Tu Huynh, Tina Marie, Sandy Maine, and Catherine Failor. And to all the talented soap crafters who have supported my business and my creative efforts through the years, especially Anna-Liese Moran.

Preface

Welcome to the world of melt-and-mold soap crafting! All you need to start your adventure is an hour or so of time, a block of premade melt-and-mold soap base, and simple cooking equipment that is easily rummaged from your kitchen cupboards.

At the end of the hour, you will have some lovely bars of soap that can be used right away — to the delight of friends and family. And the best part? Since you are working with soap, cleanup will be a breeze!

While melt-and-mold soap crafting is easy, it is also wonderfully creative. The rubber stamps, cake and candy tools, candle equipment — in short, all the jumble of creative craft materials that you have tucked away — will find fresh uses in your new hobby.

Not only is melt-and-mold soap crafting simple and creative, but the end result is also marvelously practical. Since even the most persnickety Aunt Edna appreciates a fragrant bath, soap is a wonderful gift, as well as a potentially profitable craft to sell at fairs, at bazaars, and to retail stores.

The projects in this book range from the deliciously uncomplicated to the innovative and complex. I hope that they will guide you back into "creativity kindergarten," secure in the knowledge that you can't really "mess up"; whatever your final result, it will be usable soap.

Enjoy!

1

melt-and-mold

Melt-and-mold soap crafting is a relatively new hobby that's becoming more popular every year. It's easy to see why! Soap crafting is fun, fast, and readily appreciated by those around you. As a bonus, it makes your home smell delicious and, unlike making soap from scratch using lye, it's not hazardous. Simply said, melt-and-mold soap crafting is addictive!

Soap crafting is similar in many ways to candle crafting. In candle crafting you start with a block of premade wax, then melt it down, color and scent it, pour it into molds, and allow it to harden. You follow the same steps with melt-and-mold soap, and the soap is ready to use as soon as it has hardened. But unlike messy candle wax, melt-and-mold soap base is easily washed off your countertops and out of your clothes, and kitchen utensils that you use for your projects can simply be washed up and put back into cooking service.

what makes up a soap base?

What is this miracle soap base that is so easy and fun to work with? There is no one single formula for melt-and-mold soap base, any more than there is only one recipe for chocolate cake. For this reason, the melt-and-mold soap base made by one manufacturer can be quite different from that made by another.

Generally, melt-and-mold base is either a pure soap, a blend of detergents, or a combination of the two.

Pure-Soap Bases

Pure-soap bases are made from scratch the old-fashioned way, by cooking fats and oils over heat in what is called the semiboiled method of soap making. The chemical additives are kept to a minimum in these formulations, and the soap manufacturer relies in large part on glycerin and other sugars to achieve transparency. Because pure-soap bases are high in glycerin, they are also more prone to "sweating," which is the appearance of fuzz or beads of moisture on the surface of the bar when exposed to air. On the plus side, the high amount of pure soap in these bases generally means a thicker, creamier, longer-lasting lather.

Detergent Bases

Detergent bases are made in a completely different manner, by blending various laboratory-controlled detergents, surfactants, foaming agents, and fatty acids. Detergent bases tend to be lower in sugars, and therefore they do not have the problem of sweating. Bars made with detergents are usually quick to lather, but the lather is thinner and less long-lasting than that from pure-soap bars. Some people find detergent bases to be more irritating to their skin.

Chemicals typically included in a soap base are:
- Sodium laurel sulfate or sodium laureth sulfate (SLS)
- Triethanolamine (TEA)
- Tetrasodium etidronate
- Pentasodium pentetate

If knowing the ingredients in your soap base is important to you, then you should ask your supplier for an ingredients list. Not all suppliers will provide a complete list, as these companies each guard their formula and don't want to reveal their "secret recipe" to competitors.

evaluating different bases

When I began soap crafting in 1995, there were only a handful of soap base manufacturers in North America. With increased interest in the craft, however, both manufacturers and suppliers have sprung up all over. Since there is no one formulation for melt-and-mold soap base, these folks often sell completely different products that vary in price, appearance, and performance just as widely as wines in a wine shop. Put simply, not all bases are created equal!

For this reason, I always encourage soap crafters to sample the wares of different suppliers. By comparing and contrasting raw materials in the comfort of their own kitchens, crafters will learn what to expect and what they like. The two main issues to consider are appearance and performance.

Appearance

In the world of soap making, transparency is defined as a person's being able to read 14-point typeface through a chunk of soap. To test this concept, melt down some of your soap and pour it into a mold about ¼ inch thick. When the soap is cool, pop it out of the mold and place it over the sentence below (be careful not to get your fingerprints on the soap, as these prints will make the soap appear less transparent).

Your soap is considered transparent if you can read this sentence through the soap with ease.

If you want to compare the transparency of soap bases, try reading even smaller typefaces through the bars.

Not all melt-and-mold soap base is transparent, however. Suppliers also offer opaque white base or what some call "coconut" soap bases. Usually, opaque white soap base is the same as the transparent soap base; the only difference is that the manufacturer has added a whitening agent. The most common whitener is titanium dioxide, which is often used in both paints and cosmetics.

Performance

When you use a bottle of shampoo, you have certain expectations. You expect that a single squirt of shampoo will amply lather your hair with thick bubbles and that a quick rinse will leave you feeling fresh and clean. Imagine, then, how disappointed you would be if instead it took ½ cup of shampoo to raise paltry bubbles that you had to rinse out five times! The reason this scenario doesn't happen is that shampoo manufacturers formulate their products to make sure you are not disappointed.

We also have expectations of the performance of our melt-and-mold base. Various base manufacturers are better or worse at meeting these expectations. To help you in evaluating the base, here are some suggestions:

• The base should be nearly or completely odor-free. Some bases I have tested have a smell that's reminiscent of ammonia. This unpleasant odor is unnecessary and is the sign of a poorly formulated base. It will also negatively affect the finished fragrance of your bar.

• The lather should please you. Bases high in pure soap raise a thick, creamy lather with high, long-lasting bubbles. Bases higher in detergents have a bubbly lather that is less creamy and shorter lived. Wash with a small piece of the base to determine its lathering quality.

• The soap should feel good to wash with. A nicely balanced formulation will rinse off well and not leave a thin, filmy feeling on your skin. A quality base will not leave your skin irritated or dried out.

• The base should melt easily and give you enough "working time" before it hardens up. Your soap should melt at about 140°F (60°C), and it should not harden up too quickly before you have a chance to add your fragrances, colors, and other additives.

SOAP-MAKING HISTORY

Transparent soaps were first manufactured in the late 1700s. The most famous bar from that era is Pears pure transparent soap, which is still made today. Pears developed its soap as a marketing concept by promoting the idea that transparency was the same as purity.

Pears was so successful that other companies soon copied it. By the 1920s, the number of patents filed for transparent soap formulations reached its peak; this is when the Neutrogena Corporation applied for its famous patent.

enjoy the **adventure!**

Some people are frustrated to discover that not all melt-and-mold soap bases are the same. These folks are perhaps used to working in a more established craft, where raw materials are more consistent. But in the growing field of soap crafting, new products, tools, and techniques are discovered or invented almost every day. Instead of looking for consistency, then, imagine yourself an adventurer browsing a back-alley flea market in an exotic land. Each potential purchase offers its own price, its own purpose, and its own possibilities. Explore your universe, and craft on!

2

six easy steps

Melt-and-mold soap crafting is simple: You melt the base; throw in some color, fragrance, and other additives; and then mold! Since mastering this process happens very quickly, you will soon develop the confidence and skills needed to take on — and create your own — more complicated projects.

This chapter introduces you to the basics of soap crafting. In later chapters, you will be encouraged to improve your skills through a deeper understanding of the five building blocks of soap design: color, light, fragrance, form, and function.

collecting the necessities

What do you need to get started? You can begin your soap-making adventure with just a few pieces of common equipment, which you'll most likely find in your kitchen, and some basic soap-making materials. At a minimum, you should have:

- **Melt-and-mold soap base.** For every pound of soap you purchase, you will be able to make 4–6 finished bars.
- **A knife.** Dough cutters also work.
- **A double boiler or microwave oven.**
- **A clear melting/blending bowl.** I recommend clear glass or plastic; however, any heatproof or microwavable container is acceptable.
- **Any type of stirring utensil,** such as a metal or wooden spoon.
- **Colorant** (see chapter 3 for specific ideas on what to use). How much you will need depends on how dark you want the soap to be.
- **Fragrance.** You will need 1–3 teaspoons per pound of soap.
- **Measuring spoons** for measuring fragrance. Metal is best; plastic can be damaged by direct contact with fragrances.
- **A mold** of some type. You can purchase formal soap or candy molds for your project. Or use any flexible container you have on hand, such as the bottom of a milk carton or a plastic storage container.
- **A spritzer bottle of rubbing alcohol.** I usually use the isopropyl (rubbing) alcohol found in most drugstores.

▶ Supplies and equipment, clockwise from top: scale, opaque white base, plastic molds, dough cutter, transparent base, double boiler (or microwave), cutting knife, french-fry cutter, stirring spoon, plastic molds, spritzer bottle of alcohol.

▶ Soap-making extras, clockwise from top: herbs, packaging materials, decorative ribbons, bath salts, candy thermometer, plastic containers.

Consider the Extras

Although these items aren't necessary, they are also nice to have:

- **A scale.**
- **A thermometer.** Candy thermometers are a good choice, as well as other thermometers that can measure between 80°F and 250°F (27–120°C).
- **Parchment, butcher paper, or wax paper** to work on.
- **An assortment of melting cups** to keep different colors of soap scraps in. I like to use clear glass measuring cups or other microwavable containers.
- **Bamboo skewers, dental tools, pottery tools, and other pointed objects** for stirring, poking, shaping, and nudging the soap.

- **Toys, rubber stamps, and assorted bric-a-brac** for possibly embedding into the soap.
- **Dried herbs, nutrient additives (such as sweet almond oil and shea butter), shampoo, bath salts, and other skin-pampering exotica** you have on hand.
- **Plastic containers, candy molds, PVC piping, ice cube trays, and other flexible material** that can be pressed into service as molds.
- **Plastic wrap, paper, ribbon, cellophane bags, boxes, and other fun packaging** for wrapping up your final product.
- **A notebook or recipe box** to keep track of your projects.

how to make
melt-and-mold soap

You've purchased the necessary ingredients and gathered the equipment. You've prepared your work area and arranged all of your items for easy access. So how do you start making soap?

SIX EASY STEPS TO SOAP CRAFTING

Step 1: Melt the soap base

Step 2: Add color

Step 3: Add fragrances

Step 4: Mix in other additives

Step 5: Pour into molds

Step 6: Unmold, use, and enjoy!

DETERMINING HOW MUCH BASE TO USE

Here is an easy way to figure out how much soap you will need for a project.

Fill your mold with water. Pour the water into a mixing bowl and use a piece of masking tape to mark how high the water reaches. Underestimate the amount of soap you think you will need, melt the soap in the microwave oven or in a double boiler, and then pour it into the mixing bowl. If the hot soap does not reach the line in the mixing bowl, throw in some unmelted soap; the hot, melted soap will melt down the additional chunks.

This method is even easier if you use a graduated measuring cup, because then you don't have to mark a line with masking tape.

1 Melt the Soap Base

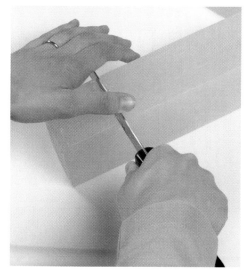

▶ **Melt.** Most people melt their soap in a double boiler or in a microwave oven. In a double boiler, melt the soap most of the way, then turn off the heat under the pot. Cover the top pot and allow the unmelted soap to gently liquefy on its own.

▶ **Cut.** Cut the melt-and-mold base with a kitchen knife, as you would cut a block of cheese. If you know how many ounces of soap your mold will hold and you have a scale for weighing the soap base, then you can cut off exactly what you need for your project. But rather than measuring exact amounts, I simply overestimate. Any extra melted soap I have at the end of the project is left to cool in the melting pot or poured off into a temporary bowl. Melt-and-mold soap base can be reheated and remelted over and over again.

▶ **If you use a microwave,** melt the soap in a heatproof bowl on high just enough to turn it into a liquid state. Be sure you use a container that is larger than the amount of soap you are using. Heat for short periods (15 to 20 seconds), stirring between each heating. It's a good idea to cover your soap while heating it.

▶ **Resin is a natural colorant that can be added during Step 4.**

Step 1 *(continued)*

▶ If you've melted the soap in a double boiler, pour it into a blending bowl. Once the soap is melted, pour it into a container that is either clear glass or see-through plastic — what I call the blending bowl. You'll use this container to add fragrances and dyes to your soap, and if the blending bowl is clear, you will be able to tell exactly what color you are producing. As you advance in soap crafting, these visual clues become very important.

> The beauty of melt-and-mold base is that it can be remelted over and over again, so you can save your "scraps" for future projects.

HEATING UP

Whatever method you use to melt your soap, don't overheat it. If you overheat the base, many problems can occur. First, you could burn it, causing your base to turn amber colored. You also run the risk of dehydrating the base, or making it waxier and less clear because it has lost moisture. If you add color or scent to a boiling-hot base, the base will immediately boil up and possibly over the edges of your blending bowl, which is hazardous. Finally, you will waste time because overly hot base causes all sorts of technical problems: It can melt embedded objects, it can warp the mold, and it will take a long time to cool down. Waiting for your creation to cool so you can unmold and admire it is the hardest part of soap crafting!

CAUTION: Hot soap is a burn hazard, just as is hot wax or hot water. For this reason, you may wish to wear protective goggles and gloves while soap crafting.

2 Add Fragrance

▶ Measure your fragrance with a measuring spoon; use 1–3 teaspoons per pound of soap (see box on page 14). Pour it into the melted soap and stir well. If you do not stir well, the finished soap will have "hot spots" of excess fragrance, which can irritate the skin.

You can scent with any "skin-safe" fragrance — your favorite perfume or fragrance oil, for example, or a pure essential oil. Don't use products that aren't recommended for direct contact with the skin, such as some potpourri and incense oils. If you have any doubt about your product, don't use it, or first do a skin patch test to check for irritation.

Because the color of the fragrance and essential oil will affect the look of your soap, I recommend that you scent the soap before you add colorants. For example, lemon fragrance oil will make your soap slightly yellow in color. If you're trying to make a blue soap, you may be disappointed to find that when you add blue colorant to your lemon-scented soap, it turns green!

GETTING THE RIGHT TEMPERATURE

To measure the temperature of your soap, pour the soap into a blending bowl and set the thermometer inside. If you want to measure the temperature while the soap is still in the double boiler, be sure to hold the thermometer away from the bottom and side of the pot so that the thermometer measures the temperature of the soap only.

Temperature	Appearance of Base
130°F (54°C)	Begins to melt
140°F (60°C)	Optimum melting temperature; soap is fully melted and should be removed from heat
180°F (82°C)	Begins to boil; although some techniques may call for hot soap, soap at this temperature will begin to discolor
250°F (120°C)	Begins to burn
Cooling Phase	
120°F (49°C)	Begins to thicken; this is a good temperature for crafting
110°F (43°C)	Forms a thick skin on top; this skin can be peeled off to reveal a thickened but still liquid soap beneath
95°F (35°C)	Reaches the gel state; can be hand-molded

HOW MUCH FRAGRANCE?

The general recommendation on how much fragrance to add is 2 percent. This means that if you are scenting 1 pound (16 ounces) of soap, you will want to add about 0.3 ounces of fragrance. If you don't work with scales, you can follow this general rule: For every 1 pound (16 ounces) of soap, use 1–3 teaspoons of fragrance. You will be able to tell whether the fragrance is too light by leaning several inches over the bowl and taking a whiff; if you smell nothing or only the barest hint of a scent, you can add more fragrance.

It is harder to judge whether the fragrance oil is too heavy, because the heat and the open bottles of fragrance will have desensitized your nose a bit. Therefore, don't exceed the recommended 1–3 teaspoons per pound unless you've made a test bar and found the fragrance to be insufficient. Too much fragrance can cloud the soap or make it irritating to the skin, and it is also a waste of money.

3 Add Color

▶ Squeeze liquid colorant into soap, bit by bit, and stir until you get the color you want. If using solid colorants, melt in a separate bowl first and then add to the soap bowl a little at a time. Alternatively, use a knife to shave off small pieces of your solid colorant directly into your melted soap. Stir until all the pieces melt into the soap. Powdered colorants can sometimes be added directly to the melted soap base. However, to avoid speckling and clumping, I recommend that you mix the powdered colorant with water in a separate container; then slowly add this mixture to the melted soap until you achieve the desired shade.

There are so many wonderful products out there that you can use for colorants (see chapter 3). Generally, soap color is available in liquid, solid, and powder form. Liquids are the easiest to work with.

4 Incorporate Other Additives

Customize your soap by adding liquid additives such as almond oil and vitamin E, or solid additives such as oatmeal and ground loofa. (See page 16 for a list of some possible additives and recommended amounts.)

▶ When adding liquids, simply measure the liquid with a measuring spoon and add to your melted soap. Stir well for about 30 seconds. How much of a liquid to add depends on what it is. If you are unsure, make a test bar using only 1 teaspoon of additive per pound of soap, and make another test bar using 1 tablespoon per pound of soap. By comparing the final bars, you will discover the best proportion. Excessive additives will make the soap cloudy, or the additives will separate out, causing uneven pockets on the surface of the bar.

Solid additives, such as oatmeal, tend to sink to the bottom of the mold after you pour the soap. If this is the look you want, you don't need to worry about it. However, if you want the additive to suspend throughout the bar evenly, you'll need to do this step a little differently. Don't pour the soap into the mold while it is still hot; rather, allow it to cool in the blending bowl, while you continuously but gently stir the soap and additive together. When the mixture thickens and begins to reach the gel stage, pour it into the mold.

When I am forming embedments, such as a jelly roll, I like to thin down the soap with liquid soap to make it malleable and give it a longer working time.

A GUIDE TO ADDITIVES

Additives alter the performance of a soap bar; use them to make soap milder, more moisturizing, foamier, harder, or cleaner. You can also use additives to help you in crafting advanced projects.

Additive	Suggested Amount (per pound of soap)	Effect	Special Considerations
Alcohol	1–4 tablespoons	Makes the soap clearer	Tends to leave behind its scent in the finished product, and can also be drying to the skin. If you add too much, the finished soap will warp and deform as it ages.
Beeswax	1 ounce	Hardens soap; makes it less clear	Beeswax has a higher melting point than soap base; melt the beeswax separately and then add it to very hot melted soap. Use caution, as the soap-beeswax mixture may be hot enough to warp your mold!
Butters and oils	Up to 2 teaspoons	Make the soap more emollient to the skin	Add sparingly; too much will simply rise to the surface of the mold and decrease lathering and clarity.
Glycerin	1–2 tablespoons	Tends to make soap clearer and more emollient, but can also make the soap stickier and sweatier	I generally use this additive only to soften soap embedments, in order to lengthen the amount of time that the soap is soft and malleable.
Lanolin	1 teaspoon	Makes the soap more emollient and slightly harder	Will cloud the soap somewhat. Too much lanolin won't incorporate well in the soap.
Liquid soap or shampoo	1–2 tablespoons	The detergents and/or soap in these products boost lather	Tends to make the soap less clear. You can also use prescented or precolored liquid soap.
Salt water (1 part salt to 2 parts water)	1 tablespoon to 1/2 cup	Makes the soap harder and less clear	If you add salt water directly to soap, it may curdle; you may need to reheat the soap gently to completely dissolve the salt water.
Sorbital	1–2 tablespoons	The best additive to make soap base clearer	Too much will make the soap sticky.

5 Pour into Molds

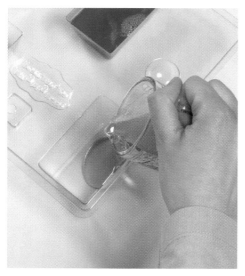

▶ Either pour the soap directly from the blending bowl or use a vessel with some sort of pouring spout. Pour directly into the middle of the mold, unless you are working with a specific advanced technique.

▶ As soon as you pour the soap into the mold, spritz the soap's surface with alcohol. The alcohol makes any unsightly bubbles vanish.

HOW TO SELECT THE BEST MOLD

You can use many items for molds. In the house of a soap crafter, nothing is sacred. The convenience of using a plastic soap mold or candy mold can't be beat, but there is also pleasure in recycling all kinds of containers from your home and pressing them into service. Some examples of good molds are yogurt containers, the bottoms of milk cartons, bread pans and muffin tins, a potato chip can, cookie cutters, and an origami box made from water-resistant wallpaper.

You will save yourself much heartache if you stick with molds that have some flexibility, allowing you to pop out the soap easily when it is hard. Plastic, thin metals, and heavy paper all work well as molds; glass and ceramics, on the other hand, are too stiff. If you want to try using a somewhat rigid mold, I recommend you first coat the mold with a release agent, such as cooking spray or petroleum jelly.

6 Unmold, Use, and Enjoy

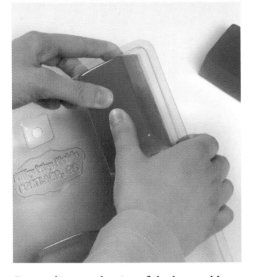

Depending on the size of the bar and how hot the base was when you poured it, your soap will be hard in 15 minutes to a couple of hours. You can tell whether the soap is hard by pressing lightly on its surface.

▶ To remove the soap from the mold, simply turn the mold upside down and press gently on its bottom. The soap should pop right out. If you have trouble unmolding your soap, it probably isn't cool enough. Try again in an hour. If the soap still won't pop out, place the mold on a hot-water bath (don't submerge the soap) in the sink or a large bowl for about 5 minutes and then try again. As a last resort, you can put the soap in the freezer for about 10 minutes, then run the mold under hot water.

AT LAST! FINISHED SOAP

Your soap is ready to use as soon as it has hardened. Once I have unmolded one of my creations, it's not uncommon for me to run to the sink for a good hand scrubbing or even jump into the tub for a soak. Washing with the soap you've created really is its final "test," and if the bar has been designed properly, you will have as much fun using it as you did making it.

If you decide not to use the soap right away, wrap the bars in plastic wrap. This prevents glycerin, which is a large part of most melt-and-mold soap bases, from "sweating." Sweating is when small beads of moisture or fuzz appear on the surface of a bar. The bar is not actually sweating out anything; rather, the water in the air is being attracted to the glycerin in the soap, and the water then beads up on the surface of the bar. If you enclose your soap in plastic wrap, you create a barrier between the soap and the air.

TROUBLESHOOTING

Melt-and-mold soap crafting is very easy, and relatively few things can go wrong.

Following are the most common problems that beginners run up against.

Problem	Why Does This Happen?	Solution
Cracking, brittle soap	Soap was overheated, lost moisture, or was placed in the freezer (or shipped in winter).	Add 5% water or 10% glycerin and remelt.
Embedments are melting	Temperature of the overpour soap is too hot, or embedments are too thin.	Adjust your technique, using either cooler overpour soap or thicker embedments.
Embedments fall out of finished bar	The embedments are not sticking to the soap.	Try spritzing embedments with alcohol before you pour base soap around them. The alcohol helps the soap and embedments adhere together. Also experiment with using a hotter overpour soap.
Embedments or additives are sinking to the bottom of the mold	Soap is too hot when you put in embedments.	Let the overpour soap cool as much as possible before molding. Try adding a tablespoon of ice water to the overpour soap just before you pour it into the mold, to cool it down more quickly.
Finished soap bar is covered with sticky liquid or a fuzzy, cotton-like texture	The moisture in the air is attracted to the glycerin in the bar and has beaded up on the surface.	Wipe down the soap with a lint-free cloth, spritz with alcohol, and wrap in plastic (see page 68 for instructions).
Soap smells funny	The soap base is low-quality or it has been overheated, causing it to burn.	Purchase soap base from a reputable supplier, and keep a closer eye on the soap temperature while heating.
Soap base has little crystalline "snowflakes" in it	The soap base is low-quality.	Try remelting the base, and then add $1/4$–$1/2$ cup of water per pound of soap.
Layered soap is splitting apart	Layers were allowed to cool for too long between pours.	The first layer should still be warm when the second is poured. You should be able to press down on its surface with your finger and feel the soap underneath "give" under the pressure. Also, liberally spritz the first layer with alcohol to help adherence.
Colors are bleeding	The colorant is water-soluble.	If this is an issue for you, switch to non-bleeding colorants. (See pages 22–27 for more information on colorants.)
Colorant makes the soap opaque	The colorant is not water-soluble.	If this is an issue for you, switch to water-soluble colorants. (See pages 22–27 for more information on colorants.)

3

using color

Every time I display my wares at a craft show, I find that customers are first attracted to the dynamic color of my soaps. Color is the first key to good soap design, and working with color is part of what makes soap crafting so much fun.

In this chapter, you will learn all about the colorants used in soap crafting: what to use, how they work, and what colors look good together. You'll learn to create designs that are fun, eye-catching, and unique. There is such a variety of colorants that you'll never be at a loss for choices. Try different types of coloring agents to determine your preferences for each project. Experimentation is often the best way to learn.

We've got a lot to cover, so let's get to work!

consider the options

Color doesn't really add emollience, mildness, or hardness to the soap, and it rarely adds scent. Perfectly wonderful bars of soap are made every day without any consideration of color. However, for the creative melt-and-mold soap crafter, working with color is a big part of the fun.

There are three basic types of colorants: dyes, pigments, and natural additives.

Dyes

A dye is a colorant that readily dissolves into the base, tinting it without making it less transparent. The beginning soap crafter will often use food coloring to dye soap. Food coloring is inexpensive, readily available, and nontoxic. But food coloring is not the only type of dye available to soap crafters. Natural plant dyes are also obtainable, such as annatto seed, osage, alkanet root, red sandalwood, logwood, and brazilwood. Stir dyes into a soap in small amounts, increasing the amounts as necessary in order to achieve the desired color.

Unfortunately, most dyes have three problems: fading, staining, and bleeding.

Fading. A soap dyed purple can look beautiful when it first comes out of the mold, only to have its color completely bleach out within a few hours or days. This is because some dyes fade when they are exposed to rays of ultraviolet light or when they interact with the pH balance of your base or other additives.

Staining. The second problem with dyes is that you can't create dark colors without using excessive amounts of dye. And too much dye causes problems. If, for instance, you make a dark blue soap using food coloring, the soap will have a blue lather and it will probably stain your washcloth and skin. Most dyes should be used only to color the soap to a light shade.

Bleeding. Another problem with dyes is that they tend to bleed. For example, if you embed a red-colored soap heart into a white bar, it will look lovely at first. But within a few hours or days, the red color will start to bleed into the white soap, making the lines between the heart and the surrounding bar fuzzy and indistinct. Color bleeding may be frustrating, but you can turn a disadvantage into an advantage by creating a soap that incorporates bleeding into its design.

Pigments

In order to avoid the problems associated with dyes, many soap crafters turn to pigments. These colorants do not fade, stain, or bleed. Pigments do not dissolve in soap base like dyes do; instead they are suspended in the base. The suspension of pigments in the base will make your soap less see-through than soap made with dyes.

Because liquid, solid, and powdered pigments can be hard to find in craft stores, beginners often turn to crayons or tempera paints, both of which are made from pigments. But I find both of these products problematic.

Crayons are made up of pigments suspended in paraffin wax. In order to melt them into your soap base, you have to bring the temperature quite high; this can be hazardous and can cause technical difficulties in the crafted soap. Also, wax is not see-through when it is hard, so when your soap cools down, the wax will make the soap cloudy.

While they are not made of wax, the tempera paints present problems similar to those of crayons: They require higher temperatures and will tend to cloud the soap.

I suggest you purchase pigments from the mail-order and Internet suppliers listed in Resources. In addition to buying basic pigments such as ultramarines and oxides, you can also purchase specialty pigments known as micas. Micas, which are used in the cosmetics industry in eye shadow and blush, offer sparkle, shimmer, shine, and depth to your soap. Since melt-and-mold soap crafting is all about working with and manipulating light, using these iridescent specialty pigments is a lot of fun.

ALL ABOUT OPAQUE WHITE BASE

Most melt-and-mold soap suppliers sell both transparent and opaque white (sometimes called coconut) versions of their base. Opaque melt-and-mold base looks something like a Dove soap bar. The opaque base is usually quite similar to the manufacturer's transparent base, except that the base has been whitened with a pigment called titanium dioxide. Titanium dioxide is a very aggressive whitener that comes in both cosmetic- and noncosmetic-grade forms.

When you're working with opaque white base, there are a number of issues to keep in mind:

▶ Titanium dioxide makes all colors look pastel. If you put dark blue coloring in your opaque soap, you will get a soft, pastel blue.

▶ Titanium dioxide is heavy, so it adds weight to the base. If you are doing any special technique, such as swirling clear and opaque soap together, you will find that opaque soap tends to sink because of its weight.

▶ Because the whitener is suspended in the soap in finely ground particles, titanium dioxide tends to give a little graininess to the soap. You won't feel the graininess when you wash, but you'll notice that it helps the soap kick up more lather more quickly.

Soap crafters sometimes complain that opaque bases result in a white dusting or speckling on the top of the soap bars. What is happening is that the white pigment is falling to the bottom of the mold because the soap base is too hot and thin when they pour it into the mold, and the titanium dioxide sinks. To avoid this problem, work with cooler temperatures. Alternatively, "cut" the white soap with some transparent soap. You can melt together as much as 1 part transparent soap to 1 part white soap and still have a white bar of soap. If you're in an experimental mood, blend 1 part white soap with 4 parts transparent soap. The final soap won't be white, but it will have an exotic pearlescence that is really stunning when colored.

Natural Additives

In addition to using dyes and pigments, the soap crafter can also turn to herbs, spices, and resins as sources for color. Browse your local health food store or ethnic grocery store for ideas. Most natural colorants will limit you to yellows, greens, and earth-toned reds and browns.

Generally, there are three options when working with natural colorants:

Liquids. Some colorants, such as chlorophyll and annatto, come in liquid form. The general rule is that soap base can take up to ¾ cup of liquid per pound of soap before it starts to lose its ability to solidify, but you should add as little as possible. When you calculate how much extra liquid to add to the base, be sure to include the fragrances and additives to that amount, if these ingredients are also in liquid form.

Powders. Natural powdered colorants aren't easily stirred into soap base, so there's a risk of clumping or freckling in the bars. Think of using powdered colorants in the same way you would use flour to thicken gravy. Rather than just dumping the colorant directly into the soap pot, pour off a little bit of the base into a smaller bowl, add the powdered colorant to the smaller quantity of base, and stir well. Slowly add this colored base to the main soap pot until you get the color you want.

Reconstitutions or infusions. Some colorants, such as henna, come in powdered form but dissolve in water. Dissolve these reconstitutable colorants in a little water first, and then add this paste to the soap base. Other colorants, such as turmeric and paprika, don't dissolve in water, but they do readily release their natural dyes. You can infuse such a colorant in water by heating it in the microwave on high for a couple of minutes. Use a coffee filter to strain out the solid material, and then add the colored water to your base. Resin is a unique case because it doesn't readily release its color into water. Set the resin in a small bowl with rubbing alcohol and allow to sit on the countertop for an hour or so. When the resin has stained the alcohol, strain it out and add the stained alcohol to your base. Avoid adding more than 4 tablespoons per pound of soap, or your bar will have a strong alcohol odor.

Of course, you can also add herbs in whole form into the soap, not just for color but also for texture and visual interest. For example, whole oatmeal added to soap base will give your final bar a wonderfully natural look and color.

creating your own designs

Now that you know what colorants are available, the next question is how to mix and match colors in order to come up with fabulous soap creations.

Some people have a natural eye for color; they just know what looks good. I, however, do not, and it took quite a bit of fumbling around looking for my glasses before I realized that there is one foolproof method for creating visually appealing soap bars: Copy the experts.

Learn from the Experts

If you take a field trip to the kitchen and bath section of your local department store, you will notice that the matching towel displays are designed around themes such as Southwestern, nautical, country, and masculine. Each theme relies on a perfect balance of color and contrast. Since the washcloth for each of these towel sets usually has a little bit of every color for that theme in it, you can purchase these washcloths and use them as a color template for your project. Not only will you end up with a nicely designed bar, but your soap will also match your chosen bathroom decor.

Washcloths aren't the only source of inspiration you can use. I collect fabric scraps of all kinds. I also thumb through magazines for images and ads that appeal to me; I glue these together in color collages. When I'm in the middle of a soap project and I need to figure out what extra accent to add to make my project really shine, I thumb through my fabric collection and scrapbooks of color ideas. The visual clues they give me are invaluable.

Give Thanks to Mother Nature

Mother Nature is also an expert colorist. She doesn't just understand the rules of color — she wrote them! Take a moment to look at one of her nearby creations. Do you spy a juniper bush out the window? Note how Mother Nature has chosen a few brilliant red berries to cluster in a larger field of deep green: perfect contrast, perfect balance. Or pick a sunflower from your garden and look into its sunny face. The dramatic black center in a backdrop of golden yellow should inspire you to choose the precise colors, tones, and amounts for your next soap-crafting project.

I find it exceedingly peaceful and pleasant to design soap around one of Mother Nature's creations. By doing so I not only end up with a project with good color balance, but I also feel as though I have placed Mother's bifocals on my nose for just a moment and honored the beauty with which she surrounds us.

Test Your Design Skills

The recipes that follow in this chapter represent a variety of soap-crafting techniques, but they all have one thing in common: They are intended to reinforce what you have learned about color. **Recipes range in difficulty from one bubble ○ (fast and easy) up to five bubbles ○ ○ ○ ○ ○ (fun but complex).**

> For the best soap design, be sure your color choices match your fragrance selections. People will be confused when they get a lemon-scented bar that is colored purple.

stickable
stackables

Stickable Stackables is a fun project to share with the young kids in your life, as it reduces the danger of their handling hot soap. Because the soap is stacked on itself, it also gives you an opportunity to teach basic color theory (the red soap on top of the blue soap makes purple!). When the kids are finished, they will be eager to toss their Stickable Stackables into the tub for a fun bathtime experience.

stickable stackables

Degree of Difficulty: ○

What You Will Learn:

Soap hardens quickly and cuts easily

Ingredients:

1 pound transparent soap base

1–3 teaspoons fragrance of choice

A few drops red food coloring

A few drops blue food coloring

A few drops yellow food coloring

Special Materials:

3 blending bowls

9" x 12" cookie sheet

Assortment of cookie cutters

1 Melt the soap base as instructed on page 11.

2 Scent the melted base as instructed on page 13. Pour equal amounts of scented base into three blending bowls. Add a different color to each bowl and stir.

3 Pour the red soap on one third of the cookie sheet. Pour the blue soap next to it and the yellow soap next to the blue. Don't worry if the colors run together a little.

4 When the soap is completely cool, use the cookie cutters to cut out shapes. Peel the shapes out of the surrounding soap with a knife. ▼

5 Remove the leftover scrap soap from the cookie sheet and remelt it, keeping the colors separate.

6 Stack several soap shapes on top of each other, using the remelted hot soap as "glue" to keep the pieces together. I like to make stacks three or four pieces high.

HOW TO USE DYES AND PIGMENTS

Pigments, like dyes, may be purchased from your soap-crafting supplier in various forms: liquid, solid, and powdered.

LIQUID DYES AND PIGMENTS are the easiest to work with, because you simply squeeze the color into the melted soap, bit by bit, until you reach the desired shade. Once you've collected several bottles of liquid colorant, custom color blending becomes a snap.

SOLID DYES AND PIGMENTS are intense "nuggets" of color suspended in a soap or stearic acid base. Cut or shave off part of the solid colorant and melt it with your soap base.

POWDERED DYES AND PIGMENTS are quite simple to use as well. Measure out a small amount of powder into a small bowl and then add an equal amount of water or hot soap. Stir well and then pour into the melted soap base.

incredible
embeddables

Embedding is something that soap crafters do a lot of. We embed all kinds of things in our soap: toys, herbs, photos, stamps — you name it! But of course the best item to embed in soap is more soap; that way you have good clean fun all the way through the last sliver of the bar.

Most of the time when you embed soap in soap, your main concern is what type of colorant to use. There is nothing more dismaying than embedding a perfect blue star in a field of red and white only to watch the blue bleed into the surrounding soap over time. For this recipe, we'll stick with non-bleeding pigments.

As with any recipe, feel free to simply double or halve the amounts as you wish, to adjust for the size of your molds.

incredible embeddables

Degree of Difficulty: ◯ ◯

What You Will Learn:
> How to embed soap into soap; the importance of non-bleeding pigments

8 ounces transparent soap base

1–3 teaspoons fragrance of choice
8 ounces white soap base

Materials:
> Wax paper, butcher paper,
> parchment, or a cutting board
3–4 cookie cutters
> Mold of choice (larger than
> cookie cutters)

TIPS FOR EMBEDDING

An embedded soap design has two elements: an embedment and an "overpour." Temperature control of both items is crucial. If the overpour is too hot or the embedment is not sufficiently cool, the two pieces may melt together and your design will be lost. To prevent this problem:

▶ Make sure the embedment is completely cool before adding the overpour.

▶ Check to be sure that the overpour is not hotter than 120°F (49°C).

▶ Spritz the embedment with alcohol before adding the overpour; this will help the two soaps stick together.

1 Melt approximately ½ cup of the transparent soap as instructed on page 11.

2 Pour the melted soap directly onto your paper or cutting board. Immediately set the cookie cutters on top of the soap. Allow the soap to cool; when cool, it will seal the bottom of the cookie cutters.

3 Melt the remaining transparent soap. Color and fragrance this soap.

4 Pour the colored soap into each cookie cutter. Allow the soap to cool. ▼

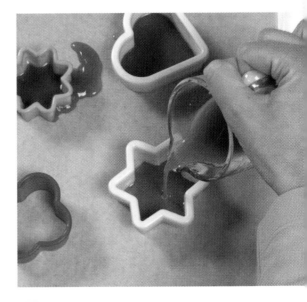

5 When cool, lift each cookie cutter from the paper or cutting board and gently push out the soap. Place this embedment facedown inside the mold.

6 Melt the white soap and fragrance it.

7 When the white soap is approximately 120°F (49°C), spritz the embedment with rubbing alcohol. Pour the white soap over the embedment. Allow to cool completely before removing the soap from the mold.

sunrise soap

In the mood for some extra sparkle? I used cosmetic-grade glitter for colorant in these bars. Glitter is heavy and tends to sink to the bottom of a batch of hot soap. Sunrise Soap is the perfect recipe for glitter because the two-handed pour technique needs much cooler soap temperatures — cooler temperatures let the glitter stay suspended.

sunrise soap

Degree of Difficulty: ○ ○

What You Will Learn:
The importance of temperature control

Ingredients:
1 pound transparent soap base
2 tablespoons yellow cosmetic-grade glitter
2 teaspoons lemon flavoring oil
2 tablespoons pink cosmetic-grade glitter
2 teaspoons cherry flavoring oil

Special Materials:
2 blending containers with pouring spouts
A four-cavity mold of choice

1 Melt the soap base as instructed on page 11. Pour half the melted soap into one blending bowl; pour the other half into the other blending bowl.

2 Scent and color the first bowl of soap with yellow glitter and lemon flavoring oil. Scent and color the other bowl of soap with pink glitter and cherry flavoring oil. Stir each mixture well.

FLAVORING OILS

In addition to the two colors in Sunrise Soap, I use two flavoring oils — lemon and cherry — whose fragrances blend together to make a "mixed berry" scent. Flavoring oils can be found in the baking section of your grocery store and in specialty supply stores.

3 Allow the soap to cool to approximately 120°F (49°C). If you don't have a thermometer, let the soap cool until a skin forms on the surface and steam ceases to rise from the top; stir the skin back into the soap.

4 Position yourself carefully over your soap mold, with a bowl of colored soap in each hand. Pour the two colors into the mold at the same time from opposite ends of the mold. If you are a beginner, work with several smaller molds; this type of pouring takes a bit of practice. If the colors immediately run together to form one color, your soap is still too hot. ▼

5 Spritz the top of the soap with rubbing alcohol to remove any bubbles. Allow to cool and harden before using.

saving face soap

The following two soaps designed by Lora Juge are born of her cold-process soap maker's tradition. These recipes are superfatted with various skin-loving oils to improve the quality of the bar. Since these soaps contain fresh plant material, they should be used up within 3 months.

I met Lora Juge in 1997, shortly after she sold her successful coffee shop in order to start up a soap and toiletries supply shop in Sacramento, California (See Resources for more information). At the time, Lora was exclusively a cold-process soap maker, or someone who makes soap from scratch with lye and oils.

Lora and I have enjoyed getting to know each other over the years, and we have come to a nice little agreement. She gets to compliment my overcomplicated soap-crafting projects, and I get to familiarize myself with her view of soap: Soap should be of a pleasing color and scent, it should be soothing to the skin, and it should honor the planet.

The avocado and carrot juice in Saving Face Soap are rich in vitamins, making the soap ideal for dry skin.

saving face soap

Level of Difficulty: ⭘

What You Will Learn:

How to incorporate skin-loving additives

Ingredients:

- 1 pound white soap
- 1 heaping tablespoon mashed fresh avocado
- 1 tablespoon fresh carrot juice
- ¼ teaspoon vitamin E
- ¼ teaspoon avocado oil
- ¼ teaspoon apricot kernel oil
- 2 teaspoons fragrance oil or essential oil of choice

Special Materials:

Molds of choice

1 Melt the soap base as instructed on page 11.

2 Immediately add all the remaining ingredients. Stir well until thoroughly mixed.

3 Pour into molds. Allow soap to cool before using.

▼ **Use vitamin E to help retard the spoilage of fresh ingredients.**

tropical
indulgence

Nourish your skin with this soap, also by Lora Juge, which contains refreshing, tropical fruits.

Wheat germ oil is a heavy, vitamin-rich oil that soothes sun-dried skin.

tropical indulgence

Level of Difficulty: ○

What You Will Learn:

How to incorporate skin-loving additives

Ingredients:

1 pound white soap

2 tablespoons coconut milk

4 teaspoons fresh banana puree

4 teaspoons fresh pineapple puree

1/4 teaspoon wheat germ oil

1 tablespoon fragrance oil or
essential oil of choice

Special Materials:

Molds of choice

1 Melt the soap base as instructed on page 11.

2 Immediately add the remaining ingredients. Stir well until thoroughly mixed.

3 Pour into molds. Allow soap to cool before using.

TIPS FOR TEMPERATURE CONTROL

It's simple to heat soap — just pop it into the microwave or warm it in a double boiler. But how do you cool it down? Here are some tips for the impatient soap crafter:

▶ Drop chunks of unmelted soap into the hot liquid soap. These soap cubes act like ice cubes, bringing down the temperature more quickly.

▶ Move the bowl of hot soap to different places on your countertop. Since the countertop under the bowl gets hot, you will speed cooling by moving the bowl to cooler spots.

▶ Set the soap in the refrigerator for a couple of minutes. I rarely do this, as I often get distracted and find the soap cools too quickly, forcing me to reheat it.

▶ Fan the soap with a magazine. (This is if you are really impatient and have nothing better to do.)

quilter's bar

There are two kinds of crafters in this world: Those who know quilters and those who *are* quilters! By the time you have finished a few melt-and-mold soap recipes, you will find that you have started to pile up scraps of soap — just odds and ends, but as any quilter knows, odds and ends can become something special.

quilter's bar

Level of Difficulty: ○ ○

What You Will Learn:
How to layer

Ingredients:
1 cup (approximately) odds and ends of soap scraps collected from other projects
6 ounces transparent soap
6 ounces white soap
2 teaspoons fragrance of choice

Special Materials:
A four-cavity or large three-cavity mold of choice

1 Rummage through your scraps and pick out colors that look good together. Non-bleeding colors are strongly recommended, but the soaps in this photo use both bleeding and non-bleeding types of colors.

2 Using a knife, cut the pieces into patterns for your design. Generally, the pieces should stand about ¼ inch high. For the soaps pictured here, I worked out two designs. The first is a somewhat structured "lone star" design, which is a classic quilting pattern, and the second is a combination of scraps that have been cut to fill a geometric pattern, somewhat like a "crazy quilt."

3 Arrange the soap scraps facedown in the desired pattern in the mold. The scraps usually stick to the bottom of the mold with a little pressure, but to help, you can use a little petroleum jelly. ▼

4 Melt the transparent overpour soap and the white overpour soap in separate containers as shown on page 11. Scent each soap with 1 teaspoon of fragrance and allow to cool to 120°F (49°C).

5 Spritz the scraps in the mold with alcohol.

Single-pour technique: If you are a beginner, I suggest you use a single overpour, as I did with the crazy-quilt design (below right). Simply pour the soap over your embedments.

Two-layer-pour technique: If you have a little soap-crafting experience, I recommend you do a two-layer pour as I did for the lone star pattern (left). The two-layer pour allows light to flood through your embedments (scraps), making them even more beautiful to look at. To create a two-layer design, pour just enough white soap to surround but not cover the embedments. Allow this layer to harden. When the white soap has hardened to the point that it feels solid but warm to the touch, spritz it with alcohol. Pour transparent soap to the top of the mold. Allow to cool and harden completely.

rainbow
loaf soap

Bring your newly learned layering and embedding skills together in a "loaf" soap, which is cast into a loaf pan. Once the soap is cool, you can slice it into individual bars. With loaf soaps, you can make a bunch of soap bars in a single project, without fussing over every individual bar. This method also allows you to spend time coming up with more complicated designs, a unique bit of which will be revealed in each sliced bar. The downside of loaf molds is that you will be working with larger amounts of soap, so if you mess up, it's a bit more disheartening.

This Rainbow Loaf Soap was designed to take advantage of the bright, see-through jewel tones of dyes, without suffering from their tendency to bleed into the surrounding white soap. The top and bottom layers of the rainbow are made out of non-bleeding pigments, while bleeding dyes in the middle layers mimic a real rainbow.

The trick to making the rainbow is to have all the soap melted and colored before you start pouring; you won't be able to run back to the microwave or wait for something to achieve the right temperature. This project isn't difficult, but it does require your full attention.

rainbow loaf soap

Level of Difficulty: ○ ○ ○

What You Will Learn:

How to make a loaf soap

Ingredients:

10 ounces transparent soap

3 dyes of choice

2 non-bleeding pigments of choice

3 pounds white soap

2 tablespoons fragrance of choice

Materials:

Several blending bowls

1 cookie sheet or dinner plate

9" loaf pan

1 Cut five equal pieces of transparent soap, approximately 2 ounces each. Place each piece in a separate blending bowl.

2 Place all bowls in the microwave and melt the soap as instructed on page 11.

3 Color each bowl of soap with a different dye. Use non-bleeding colors in two of the bowls; for the soaps pictured at left, I used ultramarine violet and ultramarine blue as my non-bleeding colors.

4 When the first pigmented soap (ultramarine violet) is approximately 95°F (35°C), pour it into the cookie sheet in a layer about 3 inches wide and 9 inches long.

5 Because the soap is cool and the layer is thin, it will form a skin on top fairly quickly. As soon as that skin is formed, spritz with alcohol and pour the next color on top. Repeat the layering process, pouring the second pigmented soap (ultramarine blue) last. Don't forget to spritz with alcohol between layers.

6 As soon as the soap has hardened but while it is still warm to the touch, peel it off the cookie sheet and immediately curve it into a rainbow shape with your hands. Allow the curved soap to cool completely.

(continued)

7 Cut two or three small pieces of white soap about ¼ inch thick. Set these pieces on the bottom of the loaf pan. ◀ Place the rainbow upside down on top of the white soap pieces; the white soap will lift the rainbow off the bottom of the mold. Some of your rainbow may stick out of the mold, but this will be trimmed off in the last step.

8 Melt the rest of the white soap. Scent the melted soap, and allow to cool to approximately 115°F (46°C).

9 Spritz the rainbow with alcohol, and then pour the white soap into the pan.

10 Allow to cool completely before unmolding. Trim any excess "rainbow" away from the bottom of the soap. Remove the soap from the mold. You may need to gently pry the soap away from the loaf pan with a knife, just as if you were releasing freshly baked bread. Cut the soap into slices as desired. A french-fry cutter creates an interesting look.

MAKING SUCCESSFUL LOAF SOAPS

Making loaf soap is fun because you never really know what you are going to end up with until you slice into your bar. There are several tips to follow when working with this technique:

▶ Always spritz with alcohol at each step to help the different layers and embedments stick together.

▶ Make sure the overpour is not too hot. If it is, it will melt the embedment and ruin the design.

▶ Pay attention to the color scheme as you build your design. A rainbow is pretty much a no-brainer, but if you decide to go for other designs, I encourage you to have your scrapbook or other source of inspiration at hand; a loaf project made with colors that aren't complementary can become muddy and confusing pretty quickly.

▶ Keep in mind the pluses and minuses of using a bleeding color.

▶ Don't bother scenting your embedments; just scent your overpour. That way, you will be able to use your scrap embedments in other designs.

▶ After you have molded the loaf, allow it to cool on its own without the aid of a refrigerator or freezer. While some soap bases can survive this rapid cooling, many will not. Cooling in a refrigerator or freezer can cause the soap layers to separate instead of sticking together. Excessive cooling in the freezer can also make the soap difficult to slice, producing shards when cut.

TIPS FOR LAYERING

Layering is the effect produced by first pouring one color of soap, allowing it to cool, and then pouring another color on top. This technique can fail in two ways: You can pour the second layer too soon, causing it to break through the first layer and create a marbling effect; or you can pour the second pour too late, causing the two layers to remain separate instead of sticking together. When someone uses the soap, the two halves will just split apart. For the most successful layering, follow these tips.

▶ The first layer should cool enough that it forms a skin on top. The skin should be thick enough to withstand the weight of the second layer.

▶ Always spritz the first layer with alcohol before you pour the second layer.

▶ Be sure the second layer isn't so hot that it melts through the skin of the first layer — 120°F (49°C) is recommended.

▶ Allow the soap to cool completely in the mold before you remove it. If you remove the soap too early, the two layers will almost always split apart, rendering useless all other careful steps.

KIDS AND SOAP CRAFTING

With proper adult supervision, melt-and-mold soap crafting can be an ideal activity for children. The two potential dangers are the cutting and the melting of the soap. To protect young children from these hazards, I recommend that an adult do all the cutting. Children should also be instructed to handle bowls of hot soap with rubber gloves to protect them from accidental spills. Allowing the soap to cool to 120°F (49°C) further reduces the risk of harm.

Once children have mastered the basics of soap crafting, there are many wonderful opportunities for projects and learning experiences. In addition to making gifts for family and friends, an enterprising child can use soap crafting as an introduction to running a business. When my nephew Solomon and his friend William were 10 years old, they spent their summer as proprietors of the Redbrook Soap Company. The boys came up with three basic soap projects and made samples of each. With the help of their grandfather, they developed an "order sheet." They then went door-to-door in the neighborhood, showed their samples, and took orders. By the end of the summer, they had cleared $70 each and had also developed a good understanding of how to run their own business.

4

controlling light

Color is one key to good soap design,
but for simple entertainment value, nothing beats the
manipulation of light. Give a small child a bar of soap with a
cool toy embedded in the middle, and he will eagerly scrub his way
to the reward. Lather up a transparent soap swirled with sea foam green,
and the thoughtless act of hand washing is transformed to meditative
wonder as the bar wears away to new colors and designs underneath.

Because melt-and-mold soap is transparent, working with it
allows you to play with the nature of light. The light that passes
through a bar of soap gives the bar depth and visual complexity
similar to the beauty of a geode or semiprecious stone.
Light is, therefore, the second building block
to good soap design.

shadow-box soap

Stack your memories in a bar of soap! A shadow box contains a montage of memorabilia set at different heights. The effect is that of a three-dimensional collage. In this recipe, images are embedded in the soap at different levels. When you look at the bar, it looks less like a two-dimensional canvas and more like a "shadow box," as the embedments are layered to create depth. While we use hand-drawn images for this soap, you can use anything, such as stickers or stamped pictures.

shadow-box soap

Level of Difficulty: ○ ○ ○

What You Will Learn:
How layering can create visual depth

Ingredients:
1 pound transparent soap
1-3 teaspoons fragrance of choice
(choose a colorless fragrance to
avoid discoloring the soap)
¼ teaspoon pigment colorant
of choice

Special Materials:
Artwork drawn on regular paper
with any drawing material
Heavy-duty, clear packing tape or
laminating paper
A four-cavity or a large 3-cavity
mold of choice
Toothpick or other small tool

1 Cut the artwork into three smaller elements (like a tree, a sun, and a house). Wrap the pieces with the packing tape or laminating material, front and back, to protect the design from moisture. Trim away any excess plastic.

2 Melt the soap as instructed on page 11.

> The last layer of the shadow box is colored to provide contrast with the foreground layers. Experiment with using more than one color in this final pour.

3 Add the fragrance oil.

4 Pour enough soap into the mold to fill it a quarter of the way. Immediately set the first piece of artwork facedown into the soap. You may need to nudge the artwork into place with a toothpick. ▼

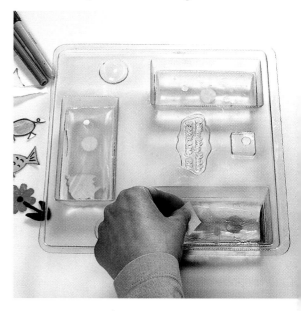

5 When the soap has cooled and is firm to the touch, spritz it with alcohol.

6 Pour more melted soap into the mold, to about the halfway mark. Immediately place the next piece of artwork facedown into the soap.

7 When the soap has cooled and is firm to the touch, spritz it with alcohol.

8 Pour more hot soap into your mold until it is three quarters full. Immediately place the last piece of artwork on top.

9 Color the remainder of the soap with the pigment. When the molded soap is firm to the touch, spritz it with alcohol and pour the colored soap on top.

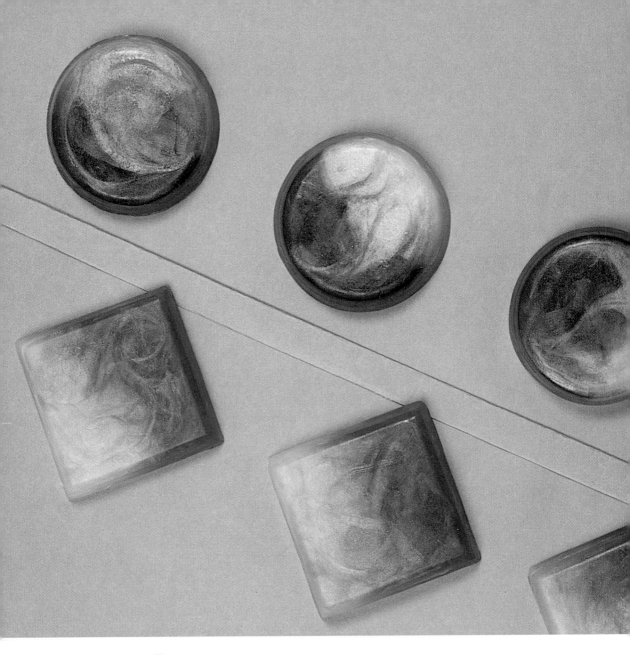

swirled soap

Elegant, marblelike Swirled Soap is very similar to Sunrise Soap (see page 33) because you work with two colors and because temperature control is all-important. The difference is that the swirls are built up in layers so that when you wash with the soap and the soap wears away, new swirl patterns are continually revealed. Because there is a fair amount of waiting between pours and because each marbled bar is unique, I recommend that you tackle at least four bars of soap at once when you use this technique.

swirled soap

Degree of Difficulty: ○ ○ ○

What You Will Learn:

How to swirl two colors together

Ingredients:

8 ounces transparent soap

8 ounces white soap

1–3 teaspoons fragrance of choice

$\frac{1}{2}$ teaspoon (approximately) colorant of choice

Special Materials:

A four-cavity mold of choice

Wide-tipped swirling stick, such as a tongue depressor or the handle end of a spoon

1 In separate containers, melt the transparent soap and white soap (see page 11 for instructions).

2 Scent each soap. Add color to the transparent soap only.

3 Allow both soaps to cool to approximately 125°F (52°C); a thin skin will form on top. Pour the transparent colored soap into the mold, approximately ¼ inch thick.

▶ **Use a variety of dried herbs to scent and add skin-healing properties to your soap.**

4 Immediately dribble a small amount of white soap in a random pattern into the soap mold. Using the swirling stick, make a few quick passes through the soap in the mold to create a marble effect. ▼

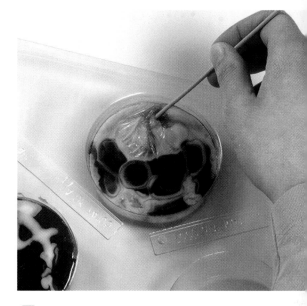

5 Allow the first pour to cool until it is firm to the touch. Spritz the surface with rubbing alcohol.

6 Pour another ¼ inch of transparent soap. Dribble in more white soap, and marble with your swirling stick.

7 Repeat this sequence until the mold is full. Allow to cool completely before unmolding.

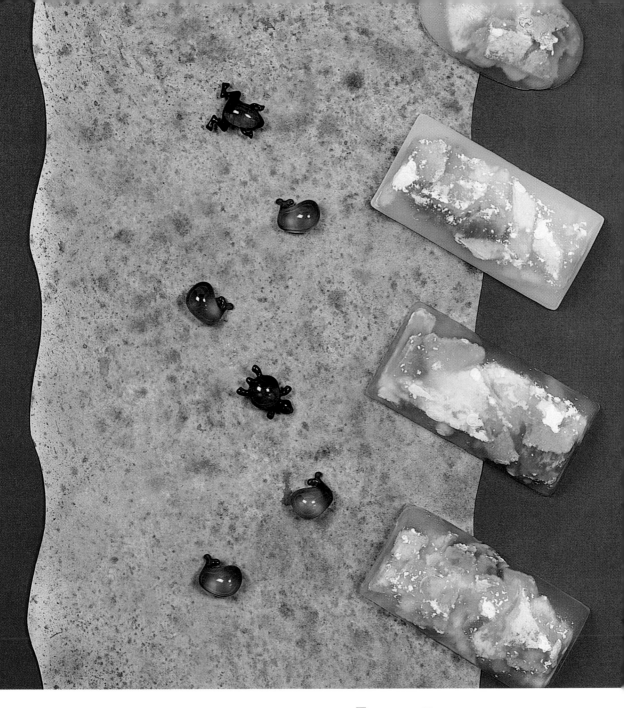

stress-relief bar

The soothing effects of bath salts in this bar will help anyone wash away stress. The finished soap looks complex because it allows for the building of light on light.

But this soap is really simple to make. While the recipe calls for a formal soap mold, you can also use a microwavable container as the mold.

stress-relief bar

Degree of Difficulty: ○ ○ ○

What You Will Learn:

When to use the freezer during soap making

Ingredients:

1 pound transparent soap

A few drops blue food coloring

½ cup (approximately) bath salts or Epsom salts

1–3 teaspoons fragrance that is similar to the scent of the bath salts

Special Materials:

A piece of aluminum foil, approximately 8" square; you may substitute with a dinner plate

Mold of choice

1 Crimp the aluminum foil so that it forms a box approximately 6 inches square and 1 inch deep.

2 Melt one quarter of the soap as instructed on page 11. Color the melted soap.

3 Pour the colored soap into the foil box and immediately sprinkle the top of the hot soap with bath salts until completely covered.

4 Place the foil box of soap in the freezer for 10 to 20 minutes.

5 Melt the remainder of the soap. Scent, but do not color, this soap. Allow to cool to about 120°F (49°C). While the melted soap is cooling, take the other soap out of the freezer. Break the chilled soap into shards ¼ inch to ½ inch square. You may also chop with a knife or cut with scissors.

6 Place the shards into the mold. Pour the cooled, uncolored soap over the shards. Allow to harden and cool completely before unmolding. ▼

USING THE FREEZER

When you're waiting for soap to cool down, the freezer beckons like a siren to a sailor. But I try to avoid using a freezer, simply because once I put my project out of sight, I tend to forget about it and leave it in the freezer for too long. While it can be advantageous to cool down embedments (making them less likely to melt into your overpour), some soap bases don't like to get too cold, and most hate to be frozen! If you use a freezer, the soap base might:

▶ Become more cloudy

▶ Become more sweaty

▶ Break into shards when you cut it, or feel crumbly

even if it is at room temperature

If you live in a cold climate and you're having soap shipped to you, be aware that you may receive soap base that has been frozen during transit. The base will have all of the problems listed above. If you receive such a base, contact your soap base supplier and see whether she has any suggestions. She may recommend that you melt down the soap with $\frac{1}{4}$ cup of water per pound of soap base in order to rehydrate it.

soap marbles

Break out of the bar and explore new shapes! This recipe introduces you to the technique of sticking together two separate halves of soap to make one complete round ball. There are actually a number of ways that you can accomplish this (see the box on page 59 for more information). To keep this recipe simple, we use tennis balls as molds.

soap marbles

Degree of Difficulty: ○ ○

What You Will Learn:
How to work with a two-part mold

Ingredients:
5 ounces transparent soap
5 ounces white soap
$\frac{1}{2}$ teaspoon fragrance of choice
1 teaspoon yellow colorant
1 teaspoon orange colorant

Special Materials:
2 old tennis balls (or 2 half-round molds for soap or candle casting)
1 plate

1 Cut the tennis balls in half with a serrated knife. Wash out the interiors with warm water and dry with a towel.

2 Following the instructions on page 11, melt the transparent soap and white soap in separate containers. Add

$\frac{1}{4}$ teaspoon of the fragrance oil to each container. Stir well to incorporate.

3 Prop the four halves of the tennis balls at an angle by resting them against an inverted dinner plate. Pour approximately 1 teaspoon of transparent soap into each ball half.

4 When the first pour has formed a skin and can take the weight of a second layer, spritz it with alcohol. Turn the ball halves so that they are resting at new angles, and pour approximately 1 teaspoon of white soap into each.

5 Color the remaining transparent soap yellow and the remaining white soap orange.

6 When the second pour has set well, spritz the soap. Tilt the halves to a new angle, and pour in about a teaspoon of yellow soap. ▼ *(continued)*

7 When the yellow soap has set, retilt the halves and pour in a teaspoon of orange soap.

8 Just before the ball halves are full, stop pouring. Set the balls upright, with open ends facing up, and fill two of them to the top with any color you choose.

9 When the soap in the two full ball halves is hard, gently remove it from the molds.

10 Reheat the last bit of soap and pour it into the two remaining ball halves. Immediately set the finished halves on top of this hot soap. Allow the soap to cool until the two halves are fused together.

11 When the soap is hardened and cool, remove it from the molds and clean any rough edges with a vegetable peeler or by running the soap balls under warm water in the sink.

Instead of using tennis balls, you can purchase professional, transparent soap molds in the half-round shape, making it easier for you to see your design as you build it.

TWO-PART MOLDS

There are several methods for making two halves of soap stick together. Here are a couple of suggestions:

▶ Pour soap into one side of the mold, allow it to harden completely, and then pop it out of the mold. Pour the other half and immediately set the first on top, making the two layers seal together (this is the method used in the Soap Marbles recipe).

▶ Slightly underpour both halves of the soap and allow them to harden. As the soap cools, an indentation will form on the surfaces of the halves. When the soap is hard, fill this indentation with hot soap and immediately place the other half on top. The hot soap will act as a "glue."

▶ Pour soap into both halves of the mold and allow it to harden. Remove the soap from the mold. Warm up a hot plate or heat a flat pan on a stovetop, and rub the bottom of each half of soap on the hot surface to melt the soap slightly. Immediately stick the two halves together.

flower power
by susan slovensky

The 1960s live on in these hot-colored flower designs. The creator, Susan Slovensky, who owns the supply company SoapBerry Lane (See Resources for more information), introduced herself to me via the Internet in late 1998. Since she lives on the East Coast and I live on the West, we didn't have any opportunity to actually craft together — an activity that always seals the friendship between soap crafters — until a year later. In the meantime, however, Susan and I exchanged photos, samples, tips, and ideas. I was quick to appreciate her talent as a designer as well as her passion for the craft. When we finally met face-to-face at the 1999 Handcrafted Soap Maker's Guild Gathering, we promptly pressed the hotel's microwave and minibar into service as a soap-crafting studio. This is a recipe Susan shared with me during our crafting session.

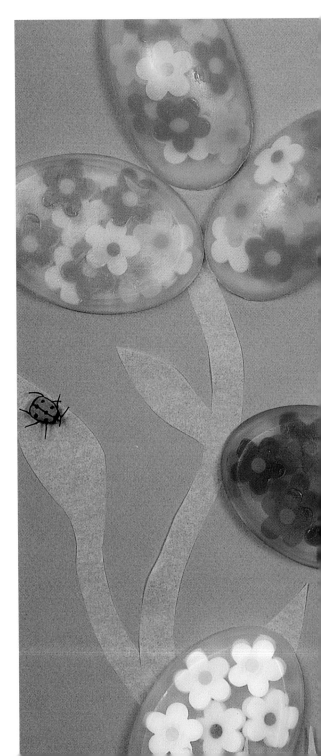

flower power

Level of Difficulty: ○ ○ ○

What You Will Learn:

How to use cake-decorating tools

Ingredients:

1 pound transparent soap

$\frac{1}{8} - \frac{1}{4}$ teaspoon neon pink gel colorant

$\frac{1}{8} - \frac{1}{4}$ teaspoon neon orange gel colorant

$\frac{1}{8} - \frac{1}{4}$ teaspoon neon yellow gel colorant

A few drops colorant of choice for the centers of the flowers

1 tablespoon fragrance of choice (Susan recommends Ocean Rain Fragrance Oil)

Special Materials:

3 blending bowls

Plastic drawer divider (or other temporary mold, such as a cookie sheet)

Flower design gum paste cutter (available at cake- and candy-decorating stores)

Drinking straw

Mold of choice (Susan uses a three-cavity, domed, oval mold)

Toothpick

1 Melt half of the transparent soap as instructed on page 11. This will become the flowers. Separate the melted soap equally into three bowls. To the first bowl add the neon pink colorant. To the second bowl add the neon orange colorant. To the third bowl add the neon yellow colorant. Stir each bowl of soap well.

2 Pour the colored soap into different segments of the plastic drawer divider to a depth of about ¼ inch. Allow to cool.

3 When the soap is cool and hard, remove it from the temporary mold. Using the gum paste cutter, cut out flower shapes. Having an odd number of flowers (3, 5, 7, or 9) in the bar looks best.

4 With the drinking straw, cut a hole into the middle of each flower

5 Lay out the flowers on a cutting board or countertop. Press down on them lightly to make sure they stick to the surface.

6 Melt a small amount of transparent soap. Color the melted soap with the colorant you've chosen for the centers of the flowers.

7 Pour the colored soap into the center of each flower. When the soap has hardened, lift the flowers off the countertop. You may need to spruce up the flowers a bit, trimming with a vegetable peeler or kitchen knife as needed. ▼ *(continued)*

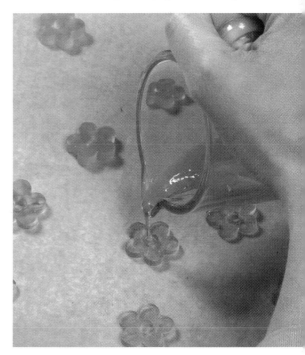

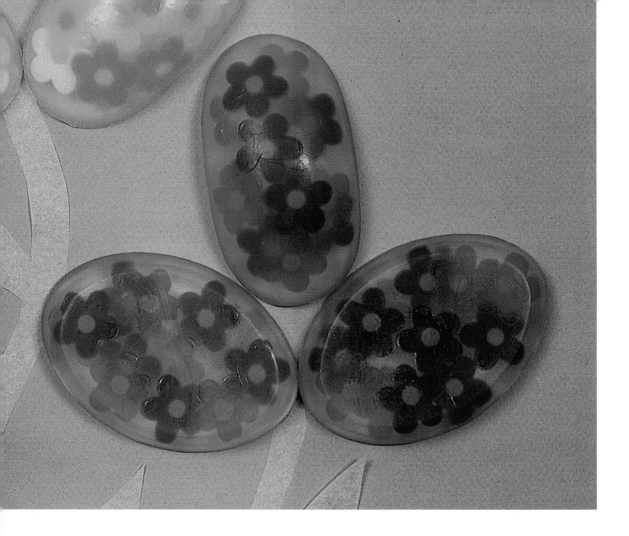

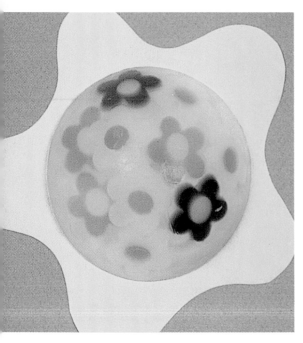

8 Melt the remainder of the transparent soap. Fragrance as desired. Pour the melted soap into the mold, filling it about one-third full.

9 Spritz the flowers with alcohol and then drop them into the soap. Adjust their placement with the toothpick. Spritz again with alcohol.

10 Fill the mold to the top with the remaining soap. Allow to harden and cool completely before unmolding.

MAXIMIZING THE TRANSPARENCY OF YOUR SOAP

In Flower Power, the transparency of the soap is a key to an attractive finished bar. Many people think that transparency is achieved by purchasing the most see-through base, but this idea is only partially true. I have worked with numerous brands of melt-and-mold soap base, and when they're crafted and packaged properly, the difference in clarity among the bases can be rather subtle.

Assuming that you are using an acceptably transparent base, here are some tips for making sure that your final soap is as clear as glass:

▶ Craft at a low temperature. If you overheat the base, you run the risk of burning and dehydrating it, both of which cause loss of transparency.

▶ Consider adding a clarifying additive, such as alcohol, glycerin, or sorbital (for more on these, see the chart on page 16).

▶ Test your fragrance for transparency in a small amount of soap. Some fragrances make soap clearer, and others make it more cloudy.

▶ Use a mold that has a completely smooth finish. If the mold has any kind of texture to it, that texture will be transferred to the soap in the form of surface imperfections, which interfere with the light waves passing through the soap.

▶ After unmolding your soap, avoid touching it with your fingers; this will prevent fingerprints on the surface. Instead, use a pencil to nudge the soap into a safe place where it can air-dry for a couple of hours. Then wrap the soap in plastic.

victorian
bridesmaid
cake

At a Victorian bridal shower, tradition called for the bride to bake a white cake for her friends. Into each slice of cake she would carefully embed silver charms, and then she would mark their placement with tiny buttercream rosebuds. The bridesmaids would find their fortunes revealed once they had eaten down to the charms.

In this version of the Victorian favorite, the cake and frosting are made from soap. To keep the project simple, I have used ribbons in place of charms, although real silver objects might be appropriate as well. Fortunes are revealed only after the soap cake is sliced into bars. For the buttercream rosebuds, I used premanufactured soap flowers, available from some of the retailers listed in Resources. However, you can come up with alternative means of marking the location of each charm.

victorian bridesmaid cake

Level of Difficulty: ○ ○ ○ ○

What You Will Learn:
How to make soap "frosting"

Ingredients:
4 pounds transparent soap
3½ tablespoons fragrance of choice
½ pound white soap
¼ cup unscented liquid soap or shampoo

Special Materials:
Colored ribbons or embeddable charms
Small cookie sheet with a lipped edge
Springform cake pan
Stick blender
Premade soap flowers
Toothpicks

1 Prepare your charms. You can purchase charms from a craft store or bead supply company, or you can make your own. For this project, I tied colored ribbons into small bows.

2 Melt the transparent soap as instructed on page 11. Scent the melted soap with 3 tablespoons of the fragrance.

3 Pour some of the melted soap into the cookie sheet, filling it to the top. Immediately place the ribbons or charms into the soap, approximately 1 inch apart.

4 When the soap in the cookie sheet is completely cool, use a knife to cut the soap into separate bars approximately 2 inches square. Each bar should contain a ribbon or charm. *(continued)*

5 Set the charm bars upright, but upside down, in the cake pan. Space them so that there is one ribbon for every "slice" of cake. If you have trouble getting the bar to stand upright, dip it in some melted soap; the hot soap will help "glue" the bar to the cake pan. ▼

HOW TO MAKE INDIVIDUAL SMALL CAKES

Instead of making a whole cake, you can make individual bars with embedded charms. Pour soap into gelatin molds and embed charms in the bottom. When the individual cakes are completely cool, you can frost them with the soap frosting described in step 8 of the main recipe.

6 Pour the remaining transparent soap into the cake mold. If you need to remelt the soap first, be sure you allow it to cool to 100°F to 130°F (38–54°C) before pouring.

7 When the soap "cake" is completely hard, remove it from the pan. Turn it over so that the side that was in the bottom of the pan faces up. Mark the locations of the charms with toothpicks.

8 Melt the white soap and scent it with ½ teaspoon of fragrance. Add the liquid soap or shampoo. Use a stick blender to whip the ingredients together. Whip until the soap forms soft peaks when you lift your blender out of the bowl. Immediately pour the "frosting" over the soap cake. The frosting will dribble over the sides and may need to be trimmed later.

9 After the frosting has hardened, remove the toothpicks and replace them with the premade flowers or other markers.

10 At the shower or party, serve the soap cake whole. Slice it into bars and give one to each guest.

> The key to this recipe is to make sure that you cannot see any charms from the outside; only when you slice open the cake is a charm revealed.

TRADITIONAL CHARMS AND THEIR MEANINGS

Here is a brief guide to some common symbols and their meanings.

Charm	Meaning
Cat	Old maid (remember, this is the "traditional" meaning; you might not want to give it to a friend unless she has a good sense of humor!)
Dime	Prosperity
Heart	Romance
Knot	Steadfastness of love
Ring	Next to marry
Scissors	Busy hands
Wishbone	Good luck

PACKAGING FUNDAMENTALS

When you wrap or package your soap, there are a couple of fundamental considerations. The first is that most melt-and-mold soaps are highly decorative, so you want people to be able to see your design. The second is that people should be able to smell the soap. Finally, because melt-and-mold soap is slightly sticky, you generally want to protect it from moisture in the air and from the smudge of fingerprints.

With these considerations in mind, you might begin your packaging design by wrapping the soap in clear plastic wrap or shrink wrap. If you work with plastic wrap, I recommend Reynolds Wrap 9/10. This grade of plastic is strong enough to be manipulated into a tight wrap, but it allows the fragrance to come through. There are many techniques for working with plastic wrap. Here is my method:

1. Tear off a piece of plastic that is 4 inches larger around than the bar of soap.

2. Set the plastic wrap on a flat surface and place the soap in the middle of the plastic, facedown.

3. Bring up all of the sides of the plastic wrap around the soap and bunch them in the middle, about 1 inch above the soap, as if you were securing a bag.

4. Lift the package off the flat surface and twist the plastic in a circle to tighten the bag. A large bubble of air will form above the soap. Use a pin or the point of a pair of scissors to pierce the air bubble.

5. Twist the plastic to tighten again.

6. Set the package back down on the flat surface. Lay the scissors flat on the soap and cut off the excess plastic.

7. Immediately place clear tape over the cut plastic to secure the package.

1 ▲

2 ▲   3 ▲   4 ▲

To package a soap in cellophane wrap or a cellophane bag: 1. Collect the materials (top); 2. Cut the appropriate length of ribbon (bottom left); 3. Place the soap inside the bag or wrapping with some straw or other packing material (bottom middle); 4. Tie the ribbon around the top (bottom right).

5

mastering fragrance

Aroma is the "goddess" of sensuality,
and it amplifies the pleasure one gets from washing
with soap. After all, when folks are using your bar, they are not
looking at it. Instead, they are tucking your creation under arms and
into the folds of bellies. If the aroma of your soap wafts toward their noses,
they will eagerly lather the bar into oblivion. Long after the soap is gone, they
will remember it and will want to buy more.

While people may be attracted to your work based on how it looks, the
ultimate test will be when they raise it to their noses for a sniff of evalu-
ation. If you have skimped on quality fragrances, or if you have
chosen fragrances that strike them as odd (a spruce essential
oil in a raspberry-colored soap, for example), they
will put down the bar and move along.

kitchen soap

This special soap is for the chef in your life. Chefs wash their hands repeatedly during meal preparation, so I have come up with a soap that is superfatted with soothing coconut and almond oils. For color, I have used chlorophyll, a natural deodorant. The French clay is a soft abrasive that helps to kick up a ready lather. For fragrance, I have blended the essential oils of rosemary and anise. These savory oils complement the activities of the kitchen, rather than detracting from them as floral or perfume oil might.

Additionally, the soaps are attached to plastic soap savers so that they will be "self-draining," allowing the master at work to plop the soaps anywhere on the countertop without fear of leaving behind a sticky mess. The attached soap saver also acts as a massager to the poor chef's hands.

kitchen soap

Level of Difficulty: ○

What You Will Learn:

How essential oils work in melt-and-mold soap base

Ingredients:

1 teaspoon coconut oil

$\frac{1}{2}$ teaspoon sweet almond oil

$\frac{1}{4}$ teaspoon lecithin

2 teaspoons rosemary essential oil

1 teaspoon anise essential oil

1 teaspoon liquid chlorophyll

1 tablespoon French clay

1 pound transparent soap

Special Materials:

5 (3-ounce soap) molds

5 plastic "soap savers" (available at kitchen and bath stores)

1 In a small container, mix together the coconut oil, sweet almond oil, lecithin, essential oils, and chlorophyll.

2 Add the French clay slowly, mixing everything into a gravy.

3 Melt the soap as instructed on page 11. Stir in the additives mixture and blend well.

4 Pour the soap to the top of each mold. Immediately set one soap saver on top of each mold. Weight down the soap saver with a cup or bowl to make sure it is fully embedded in the bar. ▼

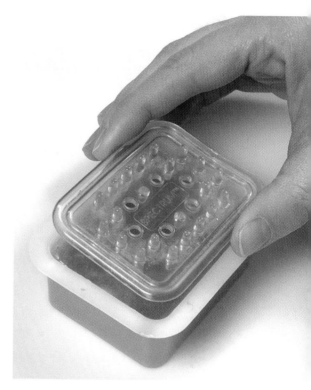

5 Allow the soap to cool and harden completely before unmolding.

JUST-FOR-FUN VARIATIONS

When I am cooking, I like to have many different types of kitchen soaps to choose from. The recipe on page 73 is for a "savory bar," for when I am working with meats and other savory items. It's also nice to have a "citrus bar" and a "sugar bar" at the ready for when I'm making fruity dishes or desserts. To make these variations on the basic theme, all you need to do is follow the main recipe, incorporating different additives.

For a citrus bar, use:

► 1 teaspoon shea butter

► 1 teaspoon sweet almond oil

► ½ teaspoon lecithin

► 1 teaspoon lemongrass essential oil

► 1 teaspoon lime essential oil

Note: The lecithin and essential oils will naturally color the soap yellow.

For a sugar bar, use:

► ½ teaspoon glycerin

► 1 teaspoon mango butter

► ½ teaspoon lecithin

► 1 teaspoon spearmint essential oil

► 1 teaspoon chamomile essential oil

► 1 teaspoon sugar or honey

Melt-and-mold soap base is an excellent carrier of aromatherapeutic essential oils because the odorless base continuously releases aroma as it is used. You can purchase a wide variety of essential oils from natural food stores, specialty shops, and many Internet companies.

raspberry and honey oatmeal
by janie gray

I once had the pleasure of visiting Janie Gray at her home in Mesa, Arizona. In addition to operating her soap-crafting supply company, Jane's Small Gifts (see Resources for more information), Janie is a true soap-crafting devotee. Her guest bedroom has become a storage area for her supplies, and her living room has been partially converted into a "soap studio," where she works her magic and offers classes.

Following are two versions of Janie's signature recipe, a special formula that she has developed, taught, and made over and over again, to the delight of family and friends. The recipe is practically foolproof, as it doesn't require careful temperature control. Make both recipes at the same time, and you can sneak off a bit of raspberries and honey to munch on while you wait for your soap to cool!

raspberry and honey oatmeal

Level of Difficulty: ○

What You Will Learn:

How additives can fall or suspend in soap

Ingredients for Raspberry-Oatmeal Bar:

1 pound white soap base

¼–½ cup old-fashioned oatmeal (not the instant type), finely ground

1½ tablespoons pureed red raspberries (fresh or frozen; thaw first if using frozen)

1 tablespoon raspberry fragrance oil
Red colorant

2 teaspoons grapefruit seed extract

Ingredients for Honey-Oatmeal Bar:

1 pound transparent soap

¼–½ cup old-fashioned oatmeal (not the instant type), finely ground

1 tablespoon raw honey

1 tablespoon honey fragrance oil

2 teaspoons grapefruit seed extract

Special Materials:

Molds of choice

1 Choose which bar you will make. Melt the soap as instructed on page 11.

2 Add all additives, fragrance, and color. Mix well.

3 Pour the melted soap into molds. The oatmeal will settle to the bottom of the molds; this is what you want.

4 Allow soap to cool and harden completely before unmolding.

SUSPENDING ADDITIVES

In Janie's recipe we want the oatmeal to fall to the bottom of the mold. But if you want the finely ground oatmeal to suspend throughout the bar, you'll need to continuously stir the oatmeal in the cooling soap. Stir slowly so that you do not add a lot of air bubbles to the bar. When the soap has thickened and is about to move into the gel state, pour it into the molds. Spritz liberally with alcohol to smooth out any unevenness on the surface that results from pouring at so cool a temperature.

oatmeal loaf
soap by joyce horton

Joyce began soap crafting in May 1997, when she wandered into a gift shop on Nantucket and saw some lovely, aromatic loaf soaps selling for $15 per slice. Within 3 months, what was intended as a hobby became a business. Joyce, who owns Aroma Fusion (see Resources), sells her finished bars to retail stores, and she has expanded into other bath and body-care products.

This is the first soap for which Joyce made her own recipe, and it has been a consistent best-seller for her. While the recipe is very simple to make, it incorporates a number of delicious-smelling, skin-loving ingredients. Since the soap includes moisturizing and sweetly fragranced additives, such as milk and honey, attention to quantities is important.

oatmeal loaf soap

Level of Difficulty: ○ ○ ○

What You Will Learn:

How to complement your fragrance with a similar family of color and additives

Ingredients:

2½ pounds (7 cups) transparent soap base

1½ ounces honey

¾ cup oatmeal (not the quick-cooking variety)

1½ pounds (3 cups) white soap base

2 ounces milk

1½ ounces bitter almond fragrance oil

Special Materials:

Square mold that can hold 2 cups water, or a clean 1-quart milk carton with the top cut off

Loaf pan, 9" x 5" x 2¾"

1 Melt 1 pound of the transparent soap with ½ ounce (2 teaspoons) of the honey. Stir until blended.

2 Pour the melted soap into the square mold. Add the oatmeal to the hot soap. The oatmeal will naturally fall to the bottom of the mold as the soap cools; this is what you want.

3 After the soap has cooled completely, unmold and slice into diagonal chunks.

4 Melt the remainder of the transparent soap together with the white soap. Add the remaining honey, the milk, and the bitter almond fragrance oil. Allow the soap to cool to approximately 120°F (49°C).

5 Pour melted soap into the loaf pan. Immediately drop the oatmeal chunks into the pan. Allow the soap to cool completely before unmolding and slicing. ▼

> **Remember to adjust the measurements of all ingredients if you reduce or increase the amount of soap base.**

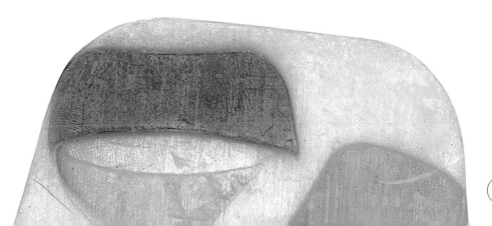

faux french milled soap

When I first started selling my soaps to stores, I had a simple way of getting in the door: I boxed up some samples, added a price list, and pounded the pavement. Up and down the streets of San Francisco I hawked my wares, leaving samples for the store buyers. These buyers were quick to assess what I offered and would either place an order on the spot or suggest another store down the street.

Sometimes, a store owner would reject my wares with the statement, "We carry only French milled soaps." To the ears of a soap crafter, such a statement is a challenge to be conquered. But how might I design a soap to look like a French milled bar? I bought some French soaps, took them home and bathed with them, and came up with the following recipe.

faux french milled soap

Level of Difficulty: ○ ○ ○ ○

What You Will Learn:
How to take an impression off a rubber stamp or other raised design

Ingredients:
3–5 ounces transparent soap

1 pound goat's milk soap (available from the suppliers listed in Resources)

1 tablespoon cosmetic-grade clay (green, yellow, or pink)

3 tablespoons milk or water

1–3 teaspoons lavender essential oil

1 ounce beeswax

Special Materials:
Sturdy paper or cellophane

Packing tape

Rubber or other stamps that are smaller then your mold

Several commercial French milled soaps with images impressed in them

Toothpicks or a dental tool

Cutting board

Petroleum jelly

5- to 6-ounce rectangular molds

1 If you're using a rubber stamp for your design, cut a strip of paper or cellophane about ½ inch tall and wide enough to wrap around the outside of the stamp. Wrap the paper or cellophane around the edge of the stamp and secure it with packing tape. This will prevent the melted soap from running off the edges of the stamp.

2 Melt the transparent soap as instructed on page 11.

3 Pour a small amount of melted soap on top of the stamp or French soap's design. Allow to cool until hard to the touch.

4 When the soap is cool, use a toothpick or dental tool to gently pry it away from the stamp or milled soap. One side of the soap will be smooth; the other side will have the design stamped into it. Lay the soap "sheet" on the cutting board, smooth side down. Repeat these steps until you have four or five stamped "soap sheets."

5 Melt the goat's milk soap.

6 In a separate container, blend the clay with the milk or water until it's the consistency of thick gravy. Spoon ½ teaspoon of the mixture into the melted goat's milk soap. Add the essential oil. Stir well.

(continued)

7 When the soap has cooled to 120°F (49°C), spritz the surface of the stamped soap sheets with alcohol. Spoon melted goat's milk soap onto them. Your intention is simply to fill in the design with some lightly colored soap. Tilt the soap sheets as necessary so that any excess soap runs off. This soap will cool fairly quickly. ▼

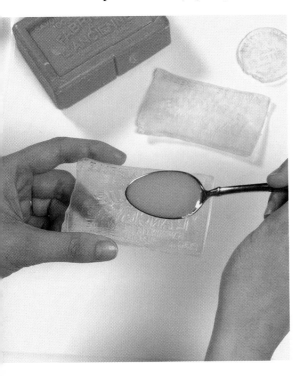

8 Smear a small amount of petroleum jelly onto the smooth side of the soap sheets. Press them onto the bottoms of the molds, smooth side down.

9 Reheat the goat's milk soap base to 150°F (65°C). At the same time, but in a separate container, heat the beeswax until it is melted.

10 Add the remaining clay and the melted beeswax to the reheated soap base; stir quickly. If you do not stir quickly, the beeswax will separate out of the soap.

11 Stir continuously until the soap is cooled to approximately 130°F (54°C). Pour the cooled soap into the molds.

12 Allow to cool completely before unmolding.

> It's fine to use French milled soaps as the "stamp" for your faux French design if your soap is meant for personal use. But if you're planning to sell your soap, you should not use a company's trademarked logo.

THE ELEMENTS OF A FAUX FRENCH MILLED SOAP

I spent a lot of time examining the design, texture, and scent of French milled soaps so that I could duplicate them in my own kitchen. So what makes one of these soaps special? These soaps must:

- ▶ Have a pretty, European design on the surface.

- ▶ Have warm, natural colors. For my recipe, I used French clays for colorant.

- ▶ Be heavier than usual. The clays I used for colorant added to the weight of the bars.

- ▶ Be harder than usual. To accomplish this, I added beeswax.

- ▶ Smell "French." Since the French are famous for their lavender essential oil, I used that.

Just to make my soaps one step above the soaps I was copying, I decided to use goat's milk soap as a base.

kaila's happy to be! bar

A professional perfumer is someone who sits down in front of his or her "fragrance organ" and concocts complicated scent blends using top, middle, and low notes from the various fragrance families. If this sounds complicated, I assure you that it is. "Noses" (professional perfumers) take their training and workmanship quite seriously.

For this reason, I am usually hesitant to try my hand at blending fragrances. But one day last year I tried a bit of blending, and I liked what I came up with so much that I had to drop everything to see whether I could extend my creative self-expression into a full-blown recipe — with consideration of all the elements of soap design: color, light, fragrance, form, and function.

This recipe gives me a great deal of personal pleasure both to make and to use. For me, both the process and the product reaffirm everything I like about myself and about life. The soap is silly, colorful, and over-complicated. I hope that you will enjoy making this soap and that someday you will also have the good fortune to develop your own Happy to Be! Bar.

kaila's happy to be! bar

Level of Difficulty: ○ ○ ○ ○ ○

What You Will Learn:
> How to outline your embedments with
> contrasting colors

Ingredients:
> 2 pounds white soap
> Blue colorant (I use TKB's
>   Blessing Blue gel tone)
> Yellow colorant (I use TKB's
>   Slicker Yellow gel tone)
> 1 pound transparent soap
> Black non-bleeding colorant (I use
>   TKB's Black gel tone)
> 2 tablespoons Happy to Be! scent
>   (blend ¼ ounce frankincense fra-
>   grance oil, ¼ ounce baby powder
>   fragrance oil, ½ ounce honey fra-
>   grance oil, ½ ounce Nag Champa
>   fragrance oil, and ⅜ teaspoon
>   raspberry fragrance oil)

Special Materials:
> A small, deep mold
> Cutting board or butcher paper
> Vegetable peeler or knife
> 9" loaf pan
> Fork

1 Melt about a quarter of the white soap as instructed on page 11. Color it yellow.

2 Pour the colored soap into the small, deep mold.

3 When the soap is completely cool, unmold it. Cut the soap into irregular shapes approximately 1 inch square. Also cut an equal amount of the unmelted white soap into similar square shapes. You will have several irregular cubes each of yellow and white soap.

4 Melt approximately 6 ounces of the transparent soap and color it black.

5 Using a spoon or your fingers, dip the yellow and white squares into the bowl of black soap and then set them on the cutting board to cool. You will have to repeat this three or four times to build up the layer of black thick enough. When you have finished coating the shapes, allow them to cool completely.

(continued)

6 Smooth out any bumps on the cooled, coated shapes with a vegetable peeler.

7 Melt the rest of the transparent soap, then allow it to cool to about 110°F (43°C). Pour the melted soap directly onto the cutting board or butcher paper. Because the soap is fairly cool, it should retain a thickness of about ⅛ inch.

8 When the soap has solidified, peel it off the board or paper and lay it in the loaf pan, as if you were working with a piecrust. Trim as needed to make the soap fit, but it doesn't have to be perfect.

◄ Poke holes all over the soap lining with the fork, just as you would poke holes in the bottom of a piecrust. Remove the transparent soap from the pan and set it aside. If it is cool enough, it will retain its shape.

9 Melt the remainder of the white soap. Scent it with the fragrance oils, and color it blue. Allow the soap to cool to 110°F (43°C).

10 Pour the melted soap into the loaf pan. Immediately drop the clear "piecrust" into the loaf pan and allow it to fall naturally to the bottom of the mold. Then drop in the cubes of colored soap.

11 Allow the soap to cool completely, then unmold and slice into individual bars.

COLOR THEORY

Most of us are familiar with the basics of color blending. We know that there are three primary colors: red, yellow, and blue. We know that red and yellow combine to make orange; red and blue combine to make purple; and yellow and blue combine to make green. But color theory extends beyond the concept of blending colors. Painting, for example, involves consideration of many other issues. I have found that two of these issues are helpful to understand in designing a colorful soap project: contrast and balance.

A low-contrast soap can be very pretty, because it is soothing to the eye. An example of a low-contrast soap would be one that is colored red and pink. Red and pink are essentially the same color — pink just contains more white. (For an example of a low-contrast soap, see Jelly Roll on page 107.)

A high-contrast soap is one in which the colors stand out because they are so different. Yellow and red, yellow and blue, and purple and green are all examples of high-contrast combinations. If you are embedding a design in soap, consider using colors high in contrast. The Quilter's Bar (see page 38) is an excellent example of a high-contrast soap.

Balance is the concept that some colors are "louder" than others, so they should be used in smaller amounts in order to achieve proper balance. For example, yellow is brighter and more intense than blue. When you make a soap with these colors, use less yellow and more blue to balance the bar visually.

According to the rules of color theory, there is not enough blue in the Happy to Be! Bar to balance out the intensity of the yellow. The yellow tends to jump out, making the overall effect slightly jarring. I've done this purposefully to reflect my personality.

If you'd like to learn more about color theory, I invite you to visit www.alpha-betcrafts.com.

6

creating form

Because melt-and-mold soap crafting is easy and fast, I sometimes feel as if I'm in a world where the rules of "what's what" don't apply. I can shape sand into castles and mud into pies, and I'm free to press sticks and cups and even my thumbs into service as I transform imagination into reality.

Deciding on the shape of the bar is a big part of the creative process of soap design. How large is it? How easily does it fit into the hand? Is it whimsical? A soap bar can take many forms — from the practical to the ridiculous — and soap designers enjoy engaging the user in their flights of form-fancy.

As you begin to develop your own recipes, you will find that sometimes you want to work a part of the soap in a free-form way. The recipes here start you out with some of the basic techniques for creating unusual soap forms.

county fair

I spied a similar cute little soap in a bag at a craft show and have since seen variations on the store shelves. This package is adorable, and it's also tremendously simple to make!

county fair

Level of Difficulty: ○

What You Will Learn:
How to suspend a toy right in the middle of a bar of soap

Ingredients:
8 ounces transparent soap
½ teaspoon clear (not tinted) fragrance of choice

Special Materials:
4" by 6" plastic or cellophane bag
Dressmaker's pin
Plastic toy that can be embedded, such as a small fish
Ribbon of choice, about 8" long

Small toys and other small embeddables are a choking hazard for young children. To be safe, use larger-size toys that cannot be squeezed into a child's mouth, and always supervise the child when he uses the soap.

1 Cut a piece of clear soap about ½ inch thick and 2 inches square.

2 Pierce the bottom of the plastic bag with the pin so that the head of the pin is on the outside of the bag and the pointed end is in the inside. Put the piece of clear soap into the bag and pierce through its middle with the pin.

3 Put the plastic toy on top of the soap cube in the bag, piercing the bottom of the toy with the tip of the pin.

4 Melt the remaining soap as instructed on page 11. Add the fragrance; then allow the soap to cool to approximately 110°F (43°C).

5 Pour the cooled soap into the bag. Immediately tie the top of the bag closed with the ribbon. Tie a knot at the top of the ribbon. ▼

6 Hang the bag of soap on a doorknob or drawer pull until it is hard. Pull the pin out of the soap. You now have a novel little gift!

bath salts box

The Bath Salts Box uses a chocolate mold to make a fun box out of soap. Use it as a decorative and aromatic container for bath salts.

The key to this recipe is to purchase a mold for making chocolate boxes. Most cake-

and candy-mold companies will have these molds in various designs. The molds often have fairly intricate floral or other patterns on their surfaces; these are fun to fill in with lots of different colors.

bath salts box

Level of Difficulty: ○

What You Will Learn:

To think of melt-and-mold soap as a casting medium instead of as a finished soap bar

Ingredients:

4 ounces transparent soap

Colorant that matches or contrasts with your bath salts

1/4–1/2 teaspoon fragrance that matches your bath salts

Special Materials:

Petroleum jelly or other mold release

Chocolate box mold

1/2 cup bath salts

1 Melt the soap as instructed on page 11. Add color and fragrance and stir well.

2 Rub a bit of mold release, such as petroleum jelly or vegetable oil, into the mold.

3 Pour the soap into the chocolate box mold.

4 Allow the soap to cool completely before unmolding; overnight cooling is recommended since the box mold is deep and can be difficult to remove the soap from.

5 Unmold the box. Fill the soap box with bath salts, and display it in the bathroom.

moldless soap

This recipe is easy, fast, and fun. I call it "moldless" soap because you simply let the melted soap cool in the melting bowl. It's a great project for the beginner or for children. The most exciting part is the moment of revelation when the soap is unmolded and cut into individual pieces. Each cut reveals a unique bar of soap. Be sure that the whole family is around for this last step!

I suggest mica colorants because they are non-bleeding and add a lot of visual interest.

moldless soap

Level of Difficulty: ○

What You Will Learn:

How to create many unique bars from the same cast of soap

Ingredients:

1 pound transparent soap

1 teaspoon each non-bleeding colorants of choice (I use TKB's Hilite Violet, Hilite Green, Neon Purple gel tone, and Neon Green gel tone)

1 teaspoon peppermint extract as fragrance

Special Materials:

1 quart-size microwavable bowl

1 plastic ice-cube tray

Toothpick or bamboo skewer

1 Melt the soap in the microwavable bowl as instructed on page 11.

2 Pour a small amount of melted soap into each of the cavities of the ice-cube tray, filling them halfway. Immediately squeeze a bit of colorant into each cavity. Stir the color into the soap with a toothpick or bamboo skewer. Place the ice-cube tray in the freezer. Allow to harden; this will take about 15 minutes.

3 When the cubes of soap are completely cool, pop them out of the tray by turning it upside down and twisting it, as if you were removing ice cubes.

4 Add the fragrance to the remaining transparent soap in the bowl and stir well. If the soap has cooled and begun to harden, reheat it briefly to bring it back to a liquid state. Immediately drop the soap cubes into the bowl. ▼

5 When the soap is cool, turn the bowl upside down and twist gently to release the soap. If you've used a glass bowl, you may have to run a knife along the sides of the bowl to help the soap release. Use a knife to cut the molded soap into bars.

TIPS FOR SLICING SOAP

When it's time to slice your soap into bars, here are some ideas for creative cutting:

▶ Use a french-fry cutter for a wavy edge

▶ Use a vegetable peeler to bevel corners

▶ Cut into "geodes" by cutting the corners off square pieces.

soap tassels

Master soapmaker Sandy Maine developed this technique. Sandy began her soap crafting over 25 years ago, making soap from scratch and selling it at farmers' markets. Today, Sandy and her husband, Louis, own and operate the thriving Sunfeather Natural Soap Company, which sells finished soaps as well as soap-making supplies.

Over the years, I have been consistently impressed with Sandy's understanding of what sells in the retail market. She is always inventing new products! Sunfeather's Soap Tassels scent the bathroom, are pretty to look at, and are quite functional, since the users simply unknot and remove a bead of soap as they need it.

Based on the color and texture of your ribbon, you will want to create four to six soap beads. These beads can be any shape, from round to triangular to square, and can be anywhere from 1 to 6 ounces in weight; don't make them less than 1 inch in diameter, though, or you will run the risk of breaking the soap when you try to thread it on the ribbon.

soap tassels

Level of Difficulty: ○ ○ ○

What You Will Learn:

How to make aromatic soap beads

Ingredients:

1 pound transparent or white soap base

1–3 teaspoons fragrance of choice

Colorant of choice

Special Materials:

1 beautiful piece of ribbon, rope, lace, or brocade, 12–18 inches long

A dowel, nail, or bamboo skewer

1 Make soap beads by one of the following methods. The first method is to dig through your scraps box and pull out soap pieces that look good together, then carve them into shapes using a knife or vegetable peeler. The second method is to pour some transparent soap into a rectangular mold and then, once the first layer cools, pour some colored soap on top. ("Bleeding" colors are good for this method, since the colors will run together.) When hard, cut the soap into rectangular bead shapes.

2 Once the soap beads are ready, drill a hole through the center of each bead using a dowel, a nail, or a bamboo skewer. ▼

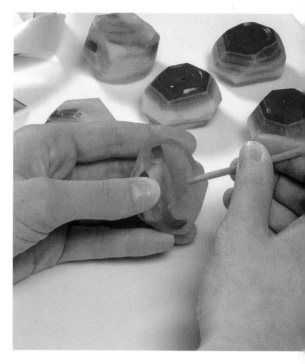

3 Tie a knot about 4 inches from the bottom of the ribbon to keep the beads in place. Then string the beads on the ribbon one by one, like a necklace. Finish off the top with a loop for hanging the tassel.

▶ **Use your imagination when displaying your soap creations.**

MAKING YOUR OWN MOLDS

Most soap crafters use loaf pans; tube molds; or assorted soap, cake, and candy molds for their creations. Sticking with these options doesn't really limit you, but you can extend your crafting into designing your own molds. Designing a mold may be absolutely necessary when you have a specific project in mind.

My preferred medium for soap-mold making is RTV silicone rubber. You can purchase this product through some soap-craft-ing supply companies, hobby stores, or specialty plastic stores. RTV silicone comes in two parts: a base and an activator. You simply stir the recommended amount of activator with the base and pour the thick, sticky liquid over the item you want to mold. Within 24 hours, it sets up to a flexible plastic mold capable of withstanding high temperatures.

For more information about making your own molds, please visit www.alphabet-crafts.com.

HOW TO MAKE "GEMSTONES"

The prettiest soap balls that I have made look like cut gemstones (see page 97 for an example.) These gems look complicated to make, but they are really quite easy.

I like to use portion cups — plastic cups that are used to hold condiments in restaurants — because of their small size. Most restaurant supply stores sell portion cups, but if you can't find them, a small plastic drinking cup will do.

▶ Step 1. Pour colored soap into the portion cups in layers.

▶ Step 2. When the soap is cool, pop it out of the cups.

▶ Step 3. Set the soap on a flat surface. Use a knife to bevel the bottom by slicing into it at an angle. Repeat all around the bottom of the soap.

▶ Step 4. Turn the soap over and bevel the top.

These gemstones are so pretty they can even be displayed on their own.

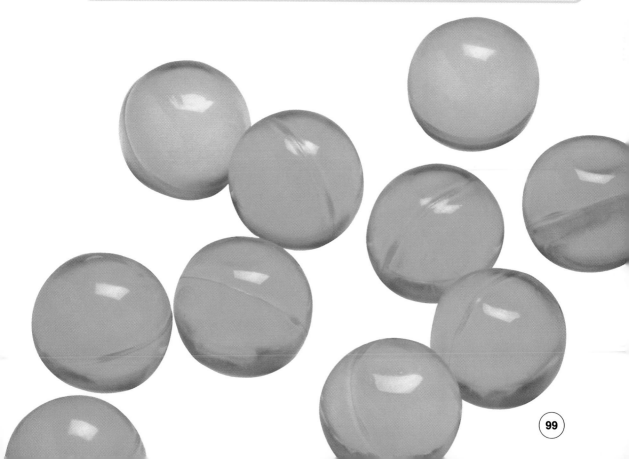

soap canes

Soaps molded in loaf pans (loaf soaps) are quite popular right now, and I am often asked how to make an intricate design run through the length of these soaps. In the following recipes, I will to teach you how to do just that by building decorative "soap canes" in tube molds. But before we jump into cane building, a little background information might be helpful.

When it comes to making a cane shape, soap is completely unlike clay or wax. If you pull on both ends of clay or warm wax, the pieces will stretch out. This is because clay and wax have long fibers that make them pliable. If you pull on the two ends of the piece of soap, however, it will break apart. Soap has short fibers and does not stretch.

Larger manufacturers of loaf soaps get around the short-fiber problem by casting soap into a long tube, such as an aluminum pipe. They then attach an industrial-grade cutter at one end of the tube. The cutter has the desired decorative shape (a wineglass, a flower, a moon, and so on). The soap is then pushed through this cutter, usually by a pneumatic press, thus creating an intricate soap cane. The cane is then embedded into a loaf soap.

Soap crafters can't duplicate the commercial cane-making method, but they have other options. They can purchase molds for basic shapes (such as hearts and flowers), or they can use tubes and rods to create canes.

Tube molds are lengths of piping into which you can cast your soap. In addition to the tube molds that are sold by soap-crafting retailers, you can also make your own tube molds from the following:

- PVC pipe
- Empty quart-size milk cartons
- Potato chip canisters
- Gutter downspouting
- Assorted plastic containers, such as lotion bottles and lip balm tubes

This is only a partial list! Whatever you use, it is important that the tube mold is open on both top and bottom. If it isn't, you will need to cut it open; otherwise you will have a hard time getting your soap out. Ideally, the tube mold would also be see-through so that you can see what you're doing as you build the design.

Rods are lengths of solid, shaped materials that can be used to create voids, or holes, in your soap. In addition to the rods sold by soap-crafting retailers, you can also use one of these items:

- Bamboo skewers
- Pencils
- Wooden dowels
- Lollipop sticks (small craft sticks)

Working with tube molds and rods to build decorative soap canes is a very interesting and challenging process, and the following projects will get you started. To learn more about how to make soap canes, I invite you to visit my educational Web site, www.alphabetsoap.com.

THE BASIC RULES OF CANE BUILDING

Cane making isn't as complex as it might seem — if you follow these golden rules:

▶ Don't bother fragrancing the cane. It adds a step to a somewhat complex process, and it makes the cane difficult to use as an embedment in other soap designs.

▶ The tube molds must be open at the top and bottom in order to facilitate unmolding.

▶ To temporarily seal the bottom of the tube mold before you begin building the cane, pour a little hot soap onto a piece of butcher paper or wax paper and then immediately place the tube on top. The soap will cool and form a seal.

▶ When you pour soap into a tube, never pour it to the very top; instead, leave about 1 inch empty at the top. This makes it easier for you to unmold later.

▶ When you set a rod into the tube mold, be sure it is at least 1 inch taller than the tube mold. Otherwise, it will be hard to get it into place.

▶ It's a good idea to spritz the different phases of the project with alcohol before doing subsequent pours, as that helps things adhere together.

▶ Always allow the soap to cool completely before you unmold it. If you don't, the different layers and sections probably won't stick together.

▶ Soak the tube of soap in a hot water bath for about 5 minutes before pushing the soap out of the tube. This makes unmolding easier.

smiley face cane

The universally popular smiley face is a great way to learn the basics of cane building (see pages 100–101 for more information). The most important thing to know is the difference between an embedment and a void. An embedment is a piece of soap that you put into your tube mold. A void is created by using a rod to make a hole, which you later fill in with soap. In this recipe, you will embed the smile and use rods to create voids for the eyes.

Since "doing" is the best teacher, let's get started.

smiley face cane

Level of Difficulty: ○ ○ ○

What You Will Learn:

The basics of building a cane

Ingredients:

4 ounces transparent soap

1 tablespoon black gel colorant
(I use TKB's Black)

1 tablespoon neon yellow gel colorant (I use TKB's Neon Yellow)

Special Materials:

1 small, empty plastic lotion tube or bottle, approximately 1" in diameter and 4" long, with at least one end cut off

Cutting board or piece of butcher paper

1 pencil

2 bamboo skewers

1 Prepare the tube mold in the manner described in the box on page 101. If you're using a tube that has only one end cut off, you don't need to seal it with melted soap.

2 Melt 1½ ounces of the soap as instructed on page 11. Pour it into a pitcher or bowl.

3 Color the soap in the pitcher black; stir well. Pour the soap directly onto the butcher paper or cutting board in a long rectangular pour, about 6 inches long and 2 inches wide.

4 When the black soap has cooled and hardened, trim off the uneven edges; you should have a rectangle that is 1 inch wide and 5 inches long. Put your scrap black soap back into the pitcher for later use.

5 Peel the rectangle of soap off the butcher paper or cutting board. Drape the soap over the length of a pencil, shaping it into a curved smile shape. Place in the freezer while you continue with the next steps.

6 Melt the remainder of the transparent soap and color it yellow.

7 Pour a small amount of the yellow soap into the tube mold at a depth of approximately ⅛ inch. This soap will act as the "glue" to hold the "smile" in place.

8 Retrieve the smile from the freezer. Set it into the warm soft soap, holding it in place until it stands upright by itself. Stick the bamboo skewers into the soap as well, arranging them as "eyes" above the "smile." ▼ *(continued)*

9 Pour the remainder of the yellow soap into the tube mold. Allow to cool and harden completely.

10 When the soap is cool, pull out the bamboo skewers. Melt the remaining black soap to a fairly hot temperature (approximately 140°F; 60°C), and pour the soap immediately into the mold. If the soap is hot enough, it will fill the eye holes readily. Allow the soap to harden.

11 When the soap is completely cool, remove it from the tube mold by gently pushing it out one of the open ends. You can stop here; but if you prefer to outline your cane with a contrasting color, proceed to the next step.

12 Remelt the remainder of the black soap. Allow it to cool to approximately 120°F (49°C).

13 Dip the soap cane into the black soap, then pull it out and let it cool for a couple of minutes. Repeat this dipping over and over again until the black outline is at the thickness you desire. When finished, the Smiley Face Cane is ready for embedding into a loaf soap or other soap project of choice.

When making canes, there are two ways to develop designs: inserting embedments and creating voids. Which method you choose depends on the shape and size of the item you're trying to make. In the Smiley Face Cane, we use an embedment for the mouth because it's difficult to find a perfectly curved item to create a void. Likewise, it's next to impossible to hand-mold a long, skinny, black "eye," so we opt for the void technique for that part.

jelly roll

Most crafters embed their decorative soap canes into loaf soaps. In this recipe, we will embed the cane into a tube-molded soap for a whimsical effect. These soaps make terrific gifts.

jelly roll

Level of Difficulty: ○ ○ ○

What You Will Learn:

How to embed a soap cane in a tube-molded soap

Ingredients:

1½ pounds transparent soap base

1 tablespoon unscented liquid soap or shampoo

1 teaspoon red gel colorant (I use TKB's Tomato Red)

¼ teaspoon white gel colorant (I use TKB's White)

1–3 teaspoons fragrance of choice

Special Materials:

Cutting board

Putty knife or dough scraper

Tube mold, 6" tall and 3" in diameter

1 Melt 6 ounces of soap as instructed on page 11, adding the liquid soap to the bowl or double boiler. Pour the melted soap into two separate bowls. Color one batch red and the other white. If you use other colors, make sure they are of high contrast.

2 Pour the white soap directly onto the cutting board. Pour in a long rectangle, about 7 inches wide and 14 inches long.

3 When the white soap has formed a skin on top, spritz it with alcohol. Pour the red soap on top of the white soap.

4 After the soap has hardened, but is still warm to the touch, trim away the messy sides with a putty knife. You will be left with a rectangle of soap approximately 7 inches wide by 11 inches long. Cut this into three smaller rectangles approximately 2¼ inches wide by 6 inches long. Roll up these rectangles into little jelly rolls. ▼   *(continued)*

5 Melt the soap trimmings in the microwave and pour directly onto the cutting board. Immediately place the tube mold upright in the melted soap; as the soap cools, it will form a seal.

6 Immediately place the three jelly rolls upright inside the tube mold.

7 Add the remainder of the transparent soap to the bowl of soap scraps and melt together. Add fragrance and stir well.

8 Pour the melted soap into the tube mold. Allow to cool completely.

9 When the soap is cool, push on the bottom of the mold to remove the soap. Slice soap into individual bars.

OPTIONS FOR CANES

Once you have made Jelly Rolls, there are several projects you can make with them. Besides embedding them into a tube-molded soap, you can lay them into a loaf pan, as in the Rainbow Loaf Soap (see page 41). Or try cutting them into 1/2-inch-long pieces and putting them in a regular soap mold, similar to the Stress-Relief Bar (see page 53).

Loaf soaps with embedments are quite popular to make, but if you are a beginner, I suggest you stick to working with tube molds or individual molds. Most loaf pans are quite large. A typical 9-inch loaf pan holds about 3 pounds of soap, so a mistake can be an expensive lesson. The most common mistakes beginners make with loaf soaps is using an overpour that is too hot; this will melt the embedments. Also, the layering technique can be tricky to master, and sometimes the different layers of color split apart when the bars are cut.

A typical 6-inch tube mold, on the other hand, stands upright and will hold about 1 pound (about four bars) of soap. Because you are pouring vertically, you don't have to fill up the mold all the way. Instead, you can experiment with making one bar at a time. You can also try different color combinations. For example, after you have set the jelly roll upright in the tube, you can melt 4 ounces of pink soap, pour it in, and allow it to cool; you can then melt 4 ounces of green soap and pour that on top. Repeat until you have four layers of soap, each a different color.

▲ By embedding jelly roll soap canes in a glycerin base, you can create a different look.

fruit canes

This recipe is slightly more time-consuming than the Smiley Face Cane (see page 103) because you will need to do several pours.

Once you've mastered the technique, you can start to design other fruits, such as kiwi and apple canes.

fruit canes

Level of Difficulty: ○ ○ ○

What You Will Learn:

How to build a cane from the inside out

Ingredients:

10 ounces transparent soap

1 tablespoon yellow colorant

1 tablespoon orange colorant

1 teaspoon lemon fragrance (or orange fragrance, if you use orange colorant)

8 ounces white soap

Special Materials:

3 round tube molds with different diameters (2", 2½", and 3" tubes are recommended)

1 Seal the bottom of the smaller tube mold as described in the box on page 101.

2 Melt some transparent soap as instructed on page 11. Color the soap yellow.

3 Pour the melted soap into the smaller tube mold.

4 When the soap has cooled completely, remove it from the tube. Use a knife to cut it into six long wedges.

5 Seal the bottom of the medium-size tube, as in Step 1. Then stand the yellow wedges upright in the middle of the mold, allowing small spaces between each wedge. ▼

6 Melt the white soap and allow to cool to 110 to 120°F (43–49°C). Spritz the yellow wedges with alcohol and then pour the white soap over them. Allow to cool completely before removing from the tube.

7 Prepare the largest tube mold as in Step 1. Set the yellow-and-white soap cane in the center and spritz with alcohol.

8 Melt the remainder of the soap and color it orange. Pour it into the tube mold around the cane.

9 When it is completely cool, remove the soap from the mold by pushing it out from the bottom. Slice it into bars.

HOW TO DESIGN WITH GEOMETRIC SHAPES

The Fruit Canes project shows you that a fruit soap is little more than six triangles grouped together to look like the inside of a citrus fruit. As a soap designer, I am often asked where one can purchase molds to make other shapes, such as stars, snowmen, trees, or flowers. Such molds are available, but they aren't necessary. I suggest that you imagine the shape you want to make as a collection of basic geometrics — triangles, squares, rectangles, and circles —and then build the design from these shapes.

For example, you don't need to use a star mold in order to make a star; simply group five triangles together, with their points facing outward. Similarly, a snowman is no more than three circles stacked on each other. A flower can be made of many shapes, such as a collection of triangles with a circle in the middle.

By sticking with bold, basic geometric shapes for your canes, you will find that it is easy to create lots of different, fun designs.

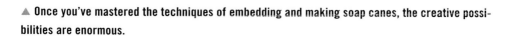

▲ Once you've mastered the techniques of embedding and making soap canes, the creative possibilities are enormous.

considering function

The concept of function, which is the last element of good soap design, is not intended to squelch your creativity; rather, it is intended to hone it, to sharpen its focus, and to bring all things together for good use. No matter how innovative you are in your soap designs, it is important to remember that you are creating not an eternal form of art, but a simple, ephemeral, and functional object: a bar of soap. For this reason, consider the purpose of the bar. Is it to heighten the senses? Provide an income? Protect the dog against fleas? These considerations are as important as any other element of design.

The recipes in this chapter are designed with consideration of their function.

gail's gals

Kids love to bathe with soaps that have toys embedded in them. But most of these soaps have toys embedded in the very middle, encouraging the child to waste the entire bar just to get to the toy. This soap is designed with the toy close to the surface so that the child will get to her prize immediately, without wasting time — or her parents' money.

Gail Matsuura and I had the opportunity to bunk together in Southern California recently during a trade show. What impressed me the most about Gail, who owns the soap crafting company C.J. Works (see Resources), was how she took her natural effervescent personality, sharpened it with her business degree, and turned herself into the "soap lady" of her hometown of Iaea, Hawaii. Her soaps, which sell extremely well, are simple in design but concept-rich. This recipe is one that I created based on Gail Matsuura's practical design suggestions.

gail's gals

Level of Difficulty: ○ ○

What You Will Learn:

That a good, practical idea will sell your product

Ingredients:

8 ounces transparent soap

½–1 teaspoon fragrance of choice

1–3 teaspoons colorant of choice

Special Materials:

Mold of choice (I use a gelatin mold)

Plastic bracelet

Toothpick or bamboo skewer

1 Melt the transparent soap as instructed on page 11. Add the fragrance oil and stir well.

2 Pour enough melted soap into the mold to fill the bottom of the mold approximately ⅛ inch deep.

3 Spritz the bracelet with alcohol to prevent any bubbles from being captured in the beads when you place it in the soap. Drop the bracelet into the melted soap and nudge it into place using a toothpick or bamboo skewer along the side of the mold. You may need to allow the soap to cool somewhat before the bracelet will stay in place.

4 Allow the first pour to cool, and then spritz liberally with alcohol to finish off the surface. Add color to the remaining melted soap and pour into the mold, filling it to the top.

5 Allow the soap to cool completely. Unmold the finished soap and wrap it in attractive packaging. ▼

Gail Matsuura emphasizes the importance of using alcohol. Not only does she spritz alcohol to remove bubbles from the surface of a poured bar, but she also uses it to help embedments stick together and to beat down skin that forms too early on a bar. She also explains that by spritzing embedments with alcohol just before you drop them in, you avoid problems with air bubbles.

shelter soap

In my soap-crafting experiments, I end up with lots of scraps and lots of mistakes. Sometimes, the scraps are so complicated with color that if I were to remelt them, I would end up with unattractive gray soap. Instead, I save all of my scraps for one grand "potpourri" bar-casting. I then take the mixed soap to my local homeless shelter, where the soap can be cut into single bars on an as-needed basis.

shelter soap

Level of Difficulty: ○

What You Will Learn:
There is no such thing as waste in soap crafting

Ingredients:
A big pile of soap scraps (enough to fill a large container)

Special Materials:
A large container, such as a 1-gallon or 5-gallon bucket

> **You can deliver Shelter Soap to the local safe house right in the bucket. Teach the shelter staff how to cut the soap into single-use bars.**

1 Sort through the soap scraps and pull out those pieces that are mostly white or mostly clear. Melt these scraps as instructed on page 11.

2 Liberally spritz the remainder of the scraps with alcohol, then toss them into the bucket.

3 Pour the melted soap over the scraps. Allow to cool completely, then pop out. ▼

fruit stand bars

Even a simple soap can be fun to make. Fruit Stand Bars are not only easy, but they also look and smell great. The best part is that you can make a large number at a time — with very little effort.

Soap crafting is an easy business to get into because it doesn't cost much for equipment, it is relatively easy to work with (and to clean up after), and it generally sells well. If you are considering going into business with your products, keep in mind that soaps are generally as inexpensive to purchase as they are to make. To put it another way, you have to sell an awful lot of bars of soap to buy a used Chevy.

There are two ways to solve this problem. The first is to make a very unusual soap and stick on a big price tag. I have a friend in Hollywood who gets away with charging $20 for every bar. The second option is to mass-produce an inexpensively made soap and sell many bars of it for a reasonable price. To sell well in volume, you'll want to make sure that your colors are vivid and your fragrances are striking so that the soaps immediately grab the attention of every potential customer.

This recipe will make about 32 bars of soap.

fruit stand bars

Level of Difficulty: ○

What You Will Learn:

Mass-production methods

Ingredients:

8½ pounds transparent soap
⅛–¼ cup bright yellow coloring
⅛–¼ cup bright blue coloring
⅛–¼ cup bright red coloring
1–1½ ounces apple fragrance oil
1–1½ ounces lemon fragrance oil
1–1½ ounces blueberry
    fragrance oil

Special Materials:

6 ft of 2"-diameter PVC
    pipe, cut into four 18"
    lengths (a circular saw
    works best for cutting this)
1-gallon plastic bucket
3 blending bowls, each able to
    hold 2 pounds

1 Melt approximately 4 ounces of soap as instructed on page 11. Pour the melted soap into the bucket.

2 Immediately stand the four PVC pipes upright in the bucket. When the soap cools, it will form a seal.

3 Set up three melting pots. Melt 2¾ pounds of the transparent soap in each melting pot. Color the first bowl of soap with yellow and scent with lemon, color the second bowl of soap blue and scent with blueberry, and color the last bowl of soap red and scent with apple. Color to a medium shade only.

4 Pour the yellow soap into the first tube, stopping 1 inch from the top. Pour the blue soap into the second tube, also stopping 1 inch from the top. Pour the red soap into the third tube, stopping 1 inch from the top.

5 In the last tube, pour in all three soaps together, either one at a time or all at once (you can later label this bar "mixed fruit"). Allow to cool for several hours; overnight cooling is recommended.

6 Once the soap is hard, fill the kitchen sink with hot water. Pull the tubes out of the bucket and set them in the water-filled sink for 5 minutes.

7 One at a time, lift out the tubes of soap and turn them upside down. Push gently on the soap at the bottom of the tube to remove it. If the soap resists unmolding, place the tube of soap in the freezer for no more than 30 minutes, and then try the water bath again.

8 Slice the soap into 3-inch-long pieces, then slice these cylindrical pieces in half lengthwise. These long half-moon shapes will make your bars look unique. Finish off the soaps with some inexpensive packaging. A piece of paper approximately 2 inches wide and 5 inches long can be wrapped around the soap in a "cigar band" style. Write the name of the soap on each bar.

the madam c. j. walker
commemorative
bar

Madam C. J. Walker was born in Louisiana in 1867, the daughter of former slaves. She grew up in the most challenging of conditions: orphaned at the age of 7, married at 14, a widowed mother at 20. Madam Walker worked as a washerwoman until she was in her late 30s, earning just pennies a day and struggling to improve life for her daughter. As she said years later, after she had become the first female millionaire in the United States, "I am a woman who came from the cotton fields of the South. I was promoted from there to the washtub. Then I was pro-

moted to the cook kitchen. And from there, I promoted myself into the business of manufacturing hair goods and preparations." It took her only seven years to build a thriving hair care company, the Madam C. J. Walker Manufacturing Company of Indianapolis.

By the time she passed away in 1919, Madam Walker was not only wealthy but had brought wealth and independence to countless other African American women by setting them up with their own salons. Madam Walker used her wealth to support and promote the rights of African Americans, and she died an inspiration to all.

The function of the Madam C. J. Walker Commemorative Bar is to remind us that any of us can promote ourselves to success and wealth — and we can also improve and inspire the lives of others.

commemorative bar

Level of Difficulty: ○ ○

What You Will Learn:

How to make a commemorative soap to honor the person who inspires you

Ingredients:

5 ounces transparent soap

¼ teaspoon fragrance of choice

½ teaspoon red gel colorant (I use TKB's Hilite Red gel tone)

Special Materials:

Antique gelatin mold (available at antiques stores) or a modern clay gelatin mold

Madam C. J. Walker commemorative stamp (originally issued by the U.S. Post Office and now available from A'Lelia Bundles; see Resources)

Clear packing tape or contact paper

1 Melt the soap as instructed on page 11. Pour approximately 2 ounces of soap into the mold and allow to cool.

2 Prepare the stamp for embedding by laminating it with packing tape or clear contact paper. Be sure it is covered on both sides. Dip the stamp in the melted soap and then lay it facedown on the cooling soap in the mold. ▼

3 Color and scent the remaining soap. Pour it into the mold, filling it to the top.

4 Unmold the cooled soap and wrap it in plastic.

The story of Madam C. J. Walker is being preserved and promoted by her great-great-granddaughter, A'Lelia Bundles. I encourage you to visit her educational Web site, www.madamcjwalker.com, to learn more about this amazing woman.

doc's fund-raiser bars

My father, Dick Westerman, designed this soap project. "Doc" is full of ideas, and he has always been interested in fund-raising crafts for 4-H, church groups, and schools (visit his Web site at www.alphabetkits.com for current projects). The idea behind this fund-raiser soap is that people love photos of others. For example, one of my customers once made soaps for a school fund-raiser and she embedded photos of the teachers in them. The soaps sold like hotcakes because every child had to have a soap with a picture of his or her favorite teacher in it.

doc's fund-raiser bars

Level of difficulty: ○ ○

What you will learn:

How to embed a photograph in soap

Ingredients:

8 ounces transparent soap

8 ounces white soap

$1/2$ teaspoon color of choice

$1/2$–1 teaspoon fragrance of choice

Special Materials:

Photos for embedding

A roll of clear, heavy-duty
packing tape or clear
contact paper

A four-cavity mold of choice

1 Gather the photos. If necessary, cut them to fit the mold. Encase each image in clear tape or contact paper, making sure to cover it completely. If you skimp on this step, the image will bleed into the soap.

2 Melt the transparent soap as instructed on page 11. Pour the melted soap into the bottom of each mold cavity until each is about one-third full.

3 Immediately place the photograph facedown on the surface of the soap. Spritz liberally with alcohol to smooth out any surface imperfections. ▼

4 Melt the white soap as instructed on page 11. Color and fragrance as desired.

5 When the colored soap reaches about 120°F (49°C) and the transparent soap in the mold has formed a skin on top, fill the mold with the colored soap. Spritz with alcohol, and allow to cool completely.

6 Unmold the finished soap.

considering function

WHAT ELSE CAN BE USED AS EMBEDMENTS?

When it comes to embedding items in soap, plastic toys are the obvious choice. But what else can be embedded in soap bars? Try:

- ▶ Baseball cards

- ▶ Pictures of sports or movie stars from magazines

- ▶ Images from religious magazines

- ▶ The illustrated animals from Aesop's fables

- ▶ Famous historical figures from children's magazines

- ▶ Stickers of your favorite cartoon character

- ▶ Wedding pictures (this makes a great anniversary favor)

- ▶ Baby pictures (a fun birthday party idea)

- ▶ Colored ribbons (such as pink, for breast cancer awareness)

Remember that you should not use someone else's copyrighted image in your soap if you plan to sell it.

▼ Plastic toys make the perfect embedment for children's soaps. Be sure toys are large enough that they can't be swallowed.

GAIL MATSUURA'S TIPS FOR MAXIMIZING SALES AT CRAFT SHOWS

Gail learned quickly at craft fairs that the real art of selling is in just getting people to stop. Since stalls are placed side-by-side in rows, people tend to walk by, scanning as they go. Only if something catches their eye do they stop to browse.

Many soap crafters display their wares by setting them flat on the tabletop. But customers can't really see the products while walking by. For this reason, Gail created a cubicle system that stacks her soap vertically. She then lines up her sliced and wrapped loaf soaps, positioning them upright. When people walk by, they see six "floors" of soap, with four rows per floor. So there are 24 soap faces in varying colors that instantly catch people's eyes.

According to Gail, scent sells. Even though she shrink-wraps her bars, customers invariably lift a bar to their noses. If they cannot smell the bar, Gail reports, they won't buy. To overcome this problem, Gail bags her shrink-wrapped soap in a plastic bag, ties it with jute, and scents the jute with the fragrance of the soap. Since she's been doing this, her sales have increased at least 100 percent.

Gail says, "With glycerin soaps, just remember that simplicity in the setup works best. The beauty is in the soaps themselves. Try not to detract from that." She also recommends talking to the customers. Find out what they like and what they are looking for. Gail offers this valuable tip: "Always tell the truth. Educate consumers when you can, and when you don't know the answer, admit it. Then take their name, do your homework, and call them back with the answer!"

Resources

Alphabet Crafts
Web site: www.alphabetcrafts.com
A "gateway" site that's a great place to learn about general crafts, including mold making, color blending, aromatherapy, and more.

Alphabet Soap
Web site: www.alphabetsoap.com
Visit my educational Web site for advanced tips, ideas, and recipes.

Alphabetsoap Kits
Web site: www.soapkits.com
This company sells soap crafting supplies to hobby and craft stores and on-line storefronts.

Aroma Fusion
Contact: Joyce Horton
Web site: www.aromafusion.net
Aroma Fusion sells a line of finished soaps to retail stores and direct to customers.

Bobby's Craft Boutique
120 Hillside Avenue
Williston Park, NY 11596
(516) 877-2499
Web site: www.craftcave.com
A mail-order resource for soapmaking supplies.

C. J. Works
Contact: Gail Matsuura
99-818 Puawa Place
Iaea, HI 96701
(808) 487-8863
Web site: www.angelfire.com/hi2/cjworks
C. J. Works supplies the Hawaiian Islands through retail stores. Gail is an excellent teacher and gives fun classes. She also sells finished soaps.

Coastal Essence
Contact: Kathy Roze
P.O. Box 242
New Aiyansh, BC V0J 1A0 Canada
Fax: (250) 633-2061
Web site: www.coastalessence.com
A mail-order supplier of soapmaking supplies and hard-to-find packaging.

Columbus Foods Company
730 North Albany Avenue
Chicago, IL 60612
(800) 322-6457
Web site: www.columbusfoods.com

Designs by AnnaLiese
1430 Northwest 11th Street
Corvallis, OR 97330
(541) 753-7881
E-mail: DesignsbyA@aol.com
Soap designer and demonstrator.

The Essential Oil Company
1719 Southeast Umatilla
Portland, OR 97202
(800) 729-5912
Web site: www.essentialoil.com
A mail-order supplier of essential oils and soapmaking supplies.

Gingham 'n' Spice, Ltd./My Sweet Victoria
Contact: Nancy Booth
P.O. Box 88SM
Gardenville, PA 18926
(215) 348-3595
Fax: (215) 348-8021
Web site: www.fragrancesupplies.com
E-mail: mysweetvictoria@hotmail.com
Bottles, bulk oils, glycerin, cocoa butter, beeswax pearls, kaolin clay, colorants, mica.

Jane's Small Gifts
Contact: Janie Gray
1909 East Dartmouth
Mesa, AZ 85203
(480) 833-8830
Web site: www.janessmallgifts.com
A mail-order soap-crafting supply company. Janie also offers classes and has done commissioned design work for manufacturing companies.

Liberty Natural Products
8120 S.E. Stark Street
Portland, OR 97215
(800) 289-8427
Fax: (503) 256-1182
Web site: www.libertynatural.com
E-mail: sales@libertynatural.com
Vegetable oils, essential oils, sulfonated castor oil, preservatives, glycerin, citric acid, dyes, containers, soap molds, melt-and-pour supplies.

LorAnn Oils Inc.
4518 Aurelius Road
Lansing, MI 48909
Mailing address:
P.O. Box 22009, Lansing, MI 48909
(888) 456-7266
Fax: (517) 882-0507
Web site: www.lorannoils.com
Vegetable oils, sulfonated castor oil, essential and fragrance oils, rosin, glycerin, citric acid.

Milky Way Molds
PMB #473, 4326 S.E. Woodstock
Portland, OR 97206
(800) 588-7930
(503) 774-4157
Fax: (503) 777-6584
Web site: www.milkywaysoapmolds.com
E-mail: sales@milkywaysoapmolds.com
Soap molds, soap stamps.

The Packaging Goddess
Contact: Charlon Bobo
P.O. Box 1806
Thousand Oaks, CA 91358
(805) 373-1076
Web site: www.
thepackaginggoddess.homestead.com
Unique mail-order packaging supplies for craft projects.

Rainbow Meadow
P.O. Box 457
Napoleon, MI 49261
Web site: www.rainbowmeadow.com
E-mail: melody@dmci.net

Self Essentials
Contact: Lora Juge
8142 A Junipero Street
Sacramento, CA 95828
(916) 388-9575
Web site: www.selfessentials.com
Mail-order soap-crafting and toiletries supplier. Store visits are welcome.

Senna's Bath and Garden
Contact: Senna Antrium
919 8th Avenue South
Nampa, ID 83651
(208) 463-4717
Web site: www.sennas.com
Mail-order soap-crafting supplier.

SoapBerry Lane
Contact: Susan Slovensky
317 West Palmyra Drive
Virginia Beach, VA 23462
Phone/Fax: (757) 490-8852
Web site: www.soapberrylane.com
Mail-order soap-crafting supplier.

Soap Saloon
5710 Auburn Blvd. #6
Sacramento, CA 95841
(916) 334-4894
Web site: www.soapsaloon.com
Mail-order soapcrafting supplies and custom molds.

Starrville Soapworks
Contact: Tom and Glinda Bauer
6180 Highway 271
Tyler, TX 75708
(903) 533-0199
Web site: www.starrvillesoapworks.com
Soap-crafting supplies available by mail order. Walk-ins are welcome.

Sunfeather Natural Soap Company
Contact: Sandy Maine
1551 Highway 72
Potsdam, NY 13676
(315) 265-3648
Web site: www.sunsoap.com
Finished soaps and soap-crafting supplies by mail order.

TKB Trading, LLC
Contact: Kaila Westerman
356 24th Street
Oakland, CA 94612
(510) 451-9011
Web site: www.tkbtrading.com
E-mail: TKBtrading@aol.com
TKB Trading manufactures colorants and molds, does custom soap design and kit manufacturing, and builds small businesses through distributorships and affiliate programs.

Index

Page numbers in *italic* indicate photographs; those in **boldface** refer to tables.

CONVERTING RECIPE MEASUREMENTS TO METRIC

Use the following chart for converting U.S. measurements to metric. Since the conversions are not exact, it's important to convert the measurements for all of the ingredients to maintain the same proportions as the original recipe.

To convert to	When the measurement given is	Multiply it by
milliliters	teaspoons	4.93
milliliters	tablespoons	14.79
milliliters	fluid ounces	29.57
milliliters	cups	236.59
liters	cups	0.236
milliliters	pints	473.18
liters	pints	0.473
milliliters	quarts	946.36
liters	quarts	0.946
liters	gallons	3.785
grams	ounces	28.35
kilograms	pounds	0.454
centimeters	inches	2.54
degrees Celsius	degrees Fahrenheit	$\frac{5}{9}$ (°F – 32)

Other Storey Books You Will Enjoy

Making Transparent Soap, by Catherine Failor. With common ingredients and equipment, you can craft stunning bars of transparent soap. Step-by-step, full-color photographs and recipes offer the perfect guide to this simple hot-process technique. 144 pages. Paperback. ISBN 1-58017-244-X.

Making Natural Liquid Soaps, by Catherine Failor. Using a simple double-boiler method, you can make liquid soaps that rival commercial brands. Includes many full-color photographs and dozens of recipes using oils, herbs, and other natural ingredients to create hand soaps, shower gels, bubble baths, and shampoos. 144 pages. Paperback. ISBN 1-58017-243-1.

The Handmade Soap Book, by Melinda Coss. Craft a wide variety of bath products from one basic recipe! Use the step-by-step instructions, full-color photographs, and ingredient profiles to create fabulous handmade soaps. 80 pages. Hardcover. ISBN 1-58017-084-6.

The Soapmaker's Companion, by Susan Miller Cavitch. This comprehensive, illustrated guide to soap making provides tips and instructions for making basic opaque bars, as well as specialty techniques for crafting marbled, layered, transparent, and liquid soaps. 288 pages. Paperback. ISBN 0-88266-965-6.

The Natural Soap Book, by Susan Miller Cavitch. Create your own herbal and vegetable-based soaps with this inspiring exploration into the benefits of chemical- and additive-free soap! 192 pages. Paperback. ISBN 0-88266-888-9.

Milk-Based Soaps, by Casey Makela. Learn how to make moisturizing milk-based soaps, such as Oatmeal and Peaches and Cream, and specialty soaps. Also included is information on how to turn this hobby into a money maker. 112 pages. Paperback. ISBN 0-88266-984-2.

These books and other Storey titles are available at your local bookstore, farm store, or garden center, or directly from Storey Books, 210 MASS MoCA Way, North Adams, MA 01247, or by calling 1-800-441-5700. Or visit our Web site at www.storey.com.